Praise for the Liptons' *Walking Easy* series

"Very thorough, organized and concise. A buy, by all means."
—Barbara Sylvia, *Senior Scene*

"Your book helped us with all the things it seemed we had to learn in a foreign country . . . I can't tell you how valuable it proved to be."
—B.D., Albuquerque, New Mexico

"We have taken our groups on many of the walks the Liptons describe, so we fully appreciate the accuracy and care they have given to their writing."
—Richard Newman, Study Tours Abroad

"It's very easy to read and very informative . . . I recommend the Liptons' book."
—Rex Burnett, *SwissTrek*

"The directions are excellent. This was our first [alpine] walking attempt, and I was very reassured to know we were on the right track."
—J.F., Sunrise, Florida

walking
easy

in the

Italian Alps

Chet &
Carolee
Lipton

GATEWAY
BOOKS

Printed in the United States of America

Gateway Books
Oakland, CA

Distributed by Publishers Group West

Library of Congress Cataloging-in-Publication Data

Lipton, Chet.
    Walking easy in the Italian Alps / Chet & Carolee Lipton.
       p.   cm.
    Includes index.
    ISBN 0-933469-22-5
    1. Hiking—Italy—Alps. Italian—Guidebooks.   2. Walking—Italy—
Alps, Italian—Guidebooks. 3. Italian Alps (Italy)—Guidebooks.
I. Lipton, Carolee. II. Title
GV199.44.I82A465 1995
796.5'1'0945—dc20   95-6503
                                          CIP

10 9 8 7 6 5 4 3 2 1

Acknowledgements

The authors wish to thank the following for their assistance and guidance:

Gianni Milani, Managing Director, Cortina Holidays; Dr. Nicolo de Sandro, Director Cortina d'Ampezzo Tourist Office; Sergio Anesi, Director Baselga di Pinè Tourist Office; Dr. Rudolph Mussner, Director Selva Tourist Office; Giorgio Cincelli, Director Val di Fassa Tourist Office; Dr. Daniela Zadra Marra, Vice Director Merano Tourist Office; Stefano Zardini, Foto Zardini, Cortina d'Ampezzo; and Kemwel Car Rental and Leasing, Harrison, New York.

A special *grazie* to the helpful personnel at the Tourist Offices in Alleghe, Baselga di Pinè, Canale d'Agordo, Cortina d'Ampezzo, Merano, Selva/Wolkenstein, Vigo di Fassa, and the Fassa Valley.

Another note of thanks goes to the hotel owners and staffs for providing the authors with local village history, general background information, and helpful hints about their best walking trails.

To Sue and Steve; Barbara, Arnie and Dustin—the next generation of *Easy Walkers*.

Contents

Becoming an *Easy Walker*   **11**

Timing Is Everything • Arriving in Italy by Airplane • Italy by Train • Italy by Car • Italy by Bus • Italy Up and Down • Italian Discount Travel • Comfortable Inns and Hotels • Enjoying Italian Cuisine • Where to Eat and Drink • Dressing for the Trail • Pack Light and Right • FYI: From Telephones to Tipping • Rules of the Road • Explanation of Symbols

Selva/Wolkenstein	**47**
Cortina d'Ampezzo	**75**
Vigo di Fassa	**103**
Alleghe	**129**
Meran/Merano	**151**
Baselga di Pinè	**175**
Venice	**199**
Accommodations	**207**
Index to Walks	**215**
General Index	**217**

BECOMING AN EASY WALKER

The Italian Alps range in a vast band of enormous peaks, encompassing the rich, green meadows of the Südtirol and the dramatic shadings and ever-changing hues of the awe-inspiring Dolomites. Walking trails in the Italian Alps match the high quality of those in neighboring Switzerland, France and Austria and are supported by helpful local Tourist Offices and sincere, friendly villagers and hotelkeepers, anxious to share the wonders of their walking paths with day-walkers from around the world. Most tourists flock to the popular Italian destinations of Florence, Rome, and Venice, too few taking the opportunity to experience the overwhelming natural beauty of the Italian Alps, to taste the local cuisine of remote villages or to share in the Ladino and Südtirol cultures.

The Südtirol of northern Italy (near the Swiss and Austrian borders) has much to offer *Easy Walkers* who are interested in the customs of this unusual area, part of Austria until it was ceded to Italy over 70 years ago. Not one but three languages are spoken—Ladin, an ancient Rhaeto-Romance language; German, a result of the Südtirol's Austrian heritage; and Italian—the reason for multi-lingual names and signs such as Selva/Wolkenstein, Sterzing/Vipitano, Klausen/Chiusa, Vigo/Vich and Ortesei/St. Ulrich/Urtejei. The high altitudes of the Südtirol are attractive to visitors, with 85% of its total area over 3300 ft. (1000 m.), ensuring cool summer evenings. The landscape appeals to those who want a wide variety of walking experiences—trails through boundless orchards and terraced vineyards, to high Alpine hamlets and remote dairy farms, to glacial lakes and tall pine forests, and to steep slopes under snow-capped peaks. From the Mediterranean climate and palm trees in elegant Merano to the cool, high, jagged Dolomite peaks at the Sella Pass, the Südtirol in Italy's northern alps has an abundance of well-signed, diverse walking trails that will thrill *Easy Walkers*.

The Dolomites, Europe's most dramatic and spectacular mountain range, lie mostly within the Südtirol. The Dolomites are composed of over 14 different mountain chains, separated by passes, valleys and rivers, with at least one 10,000-foot peak in each *massif*. They differ from the mountains in other alpine regions because of the composition of their rock. This ancient sea has been transformed by time, ice and water into peaks and ridges that have been frequently photographed, painted, explored and described. These are majestic, pale mountains with unforgettable names—Cinque Torri and Tre Cimi near Cortina d'Ampezzo, the wall of Civetta towering over Alleghe, the mighty Sassolungo across from Selva, and Catinaccio/Rosengarten working its magic spell above Vigo di Fassa—and all are *Walking Easy* base villages.

The marks of history are everywhere in the Italian Alps—80 of the 350 Gothic-style castles, fortresses, manor houses and monastaries in the Südtirol, dating from the 12th and 13th centuries, are still inhabited, and several of the walks in this guidebook take you through their gates to evoke visions of knights in shining armour and bygone eras. It is enlightening to visit a museum in a large city with artifacts presented behind glass cases, but the experience of entering a furnished, occupied castle or church on the spot it was erected 600 years ago, is a very real and personal experience. *Easy Walkers* can do it all, especially in the Italian Alps; you will walk in these impressive mountains, and touch a little bit of history along the way.

Winter sports are the basis of many thriving northern Italian economies, and fabulous summer hiking possibilities attract walkers from around the world to many of the same villages, keeping the hotels filled during the shorter summer season. Strategically placed lifts bring visitors to the beginning of pleasant day-hikes through pine and larch forests on well-marked trails. *Ristorantes* and *rifugios* are everywhere, with their owners anxious to prepare local gourmet specialties that have been a part of their family traditions for generations.

Walking Easy in the Italian Alps, like its predecessors in the *Walking Easy* series, is a how-to-book, devoted to each area's most beautiful walks. These can be completed in one day by recreational walkers, who may return to their comfortable hotels each afternoon. It is recommended that *Easy Walkers* spend at least one week in each location, establishing a base village from where the walks can be reached. The base villages we have chosen and presented here are Alleghe, Baselga di Pinè, Cortina d'Ampezzo, Merano, Selva, and Vigo di Fassa. Merano and Selva are located in the Südtirol; Alleghe, Cortina, Selva and Vigo are in the Dolomites; and Baselga is in the southern alps. All beckon you to discover the varied delights of *Walking Easy in the Italian Alps*. As a bonus for *Easy Walkers,* a short walking tour of historical, romantic Venice is included, only a two- to three-hour ride from many Italian alpine areas.

Walking Easy in the Italian Alps includes a brief description of each base village, the use of public and automobile transportation, local activities and attractions, excursions to nearby points of interest, and most importantly, detailed instructions and "easy-guide" maps for day walks. Every activity has been experienced by the authors to better evaluate the needs of active adult recreational walkers and their families. Each walk in this guidebook is preceded by a description of its location, followed by directions on how to arrive at the start of the walk from the base village. Many walks begin with a mountain railway or thrilling cable car ride, while others are gentle walks through the forest or around a lake. Some are above the treeline, others descend through alpine meadows. Unless specifically mentioned, the paths are well-maintained and well-signed.

Each walk is graded into one of three classifications: **gentle**, low-level walks with few ascents and descents, through valleys, around lakes and along rivers; **comfortable**, ascents and descents over mixed terrain; **more challenging**, longer, more challenging ascents and descents on narrower trails.

All walks can be accomplished in two to five hours, by recreational walkers of any age in good health. In addition to the "easy-guide" maps of each walk, you will also find a recommended hiking map listed at the beginning of each village's **Walks** section. These and other maps can be purchased at local Tourist Information offices or newspaper/magazine stores. While a map is a necessity, you may also find it fun to carry a small, inexpensive compass to check directions and a pedometer to keep track of walking distances.

The "walking time" listed before each walk is time spent actually walking. It does **not** include time spent for lunch, resting, photography, scenery breaks, sightseeing and transportation. This additional time is left to the discretion of each *Easy Walker*, so that an average day with a three-hour walk usually begins at 9:00 or 10:00 am and ends back at your hotel in the late afternoon.

The Italian Alps have hundreds of miles of trails, most well-signed and easily followed. As in the earlier *Walking Easy* series guidebooks on Switzerland, Austria and France, the paths in the Italian Alps were chosen for their beauty, accessibility, walking time and ease of use. But, be warned—**not** all the hikes are easy. Many will joyously challenge your capabilities with ascents and descents over mixed terrain. However, it is not uncommon for people of all ages to be steadily wending their way along favorite trails. Walking is not just for the young, it is also for the young at heart. The Italians have created a wonderful trail system in the alps and it is the best way to see the magnificent countryside—walkers are welcome almost everywhere in their hiking boots and backpacks.

You can do it—just tuck a copy of *Walking Easy in the Italian Alps* in a pocket and you are on your way!

Timing Is Everything

The villages in the Dolomites are warmer and have less annual rainfall than the northern alpine areas in Switzerland and Austria. Hiking season here can begin at the end of June and last through the end of September. Mid-June to early August features pleasant days and cool nights, with little rain. The days become warmer in August with late afternoon showers not uncommon. However, September is usually clear and pleasant, continuing into the beginning of October.

If you have a choice of selecting the timing of your walking vacation, the end of June and the beginning of September are superior—there are fewer tourists and a cooler climate—ideal for walking. July and August, although warmer and more crowded, feature brilliant explosions of wildflowers throughout the alps and their valleys. While the cities are busy with European summer vacationers, the serenity of thousands of miles of shaded forest and high alpine trails is hardly ever shattered by too many walkers. Although the trails are usually uncrowded, remember that in August almost all of Italy goes on vacation, especially around the August 15th national holiday of Ferragosto. Vacationing Italians descend upon the roads and the trains—don't leave home without reservations! Note also that many lifts do not open until July 1 and others may close about September 15. Always check with the Tourist Office in the base villages to be sure lifts are running and plan your walking trip accordingly.

Snow can cover some of the higher trails in June, but the riotous colors of alpine meadow flowers, framed against the white mountain peaks, are breathtaking. The unusual color intensity of alpine blooms comes from their absorption of the sun's strong ultraviolet rays at higher altitudes, and the moisture and soil in the Italian alps are ideal for wildflowers. Crocus peek out from the remaining snow in the spring, and in July the flowers are a rainbow of color: yellow arnicas and poppies, blue gentian, pink and red rhododendron and azalea, white edelweiss and miniature lilies. (Of course, many of these fragile alpine flowers are protected by law. To be safe, please do not pick any.) Still, we prefer the beginning of September, with cloudless blue skies the norm. However, by then the snow has melted from all but the highest mountain peaks and the meadow flowers are now dried pods, blowing in the fields. Whichever month you choose, *Walking Easy in the Italian Alps* will provide an exhilarating vacation.

Arriving in Italy by Airplane

Depending on whether or not you wish to fly directly into Italy, Milan and Munich, Germany, are the two major international airports closest to the *Walking Easy* alpine base villages. If you don't mind changing planes, the Venice airport is only two to three hours from many of our favorite mountain villages by rental car. From Milan it takes four to five hours driving time to reach the general area of the alps, from Munich about three and one-half to four and one-half hours. Train and bus service from these airports to towns and villages in the Italian Alps should be checked carefully.

Italy by Train

The Italian rail system is run by **"Ferrovie Italiene delle Stato" (FS)**. Five types of trains make up the rail service:

1) TEE or **Trans Europ Express** - Luxury, first-class only trains which run between major European cities. There is a supplementary charge for these trains, and a seat reservation is necessary.

2) Rapido - Fast, first-class trains between major cities and towns, with a supplementary charge.

3) Espresso - Long distance trains with first- and second-class cars, stopping at main stations only.

4) Diretto - First- and second-class cars, stopping at most stations.

5) Locale - Short distance trains, most second-class only, with basic comforts, stopping at all stations along the route.

Within this rail service, Italy has four types of fast trains:

Pendolino - A first-class only train which tilts, using the motion of a pendulum, to accommodate curves at very high speed. Their fare supplement includes seat reservations and a meal.

EuroCity - Express trains between major European and Italian cities; reservations are required.

Intercity - Like the EuroCity, but with more stops, reservations are required on most of these trains, but few offer full meal services.

Rapido - First- and second-class service between main stations in Italy.

Many European and Italian cities have convenient train service into larger towns and cities bordering the Italian Alps. Major railroad lines run north and south over the Brenner Pass and connect Italy with Austria and Germany. The main railroad stations in the Dolomites are at Bolzano, Trento and Bressanone, with smaller connecting lines going into Ora, Chiusa and Mezzocorona.

> ☞ **HINT: The Bolzano to Brennaro route through the Dolomites is one of the most scenic railroad trips in all of Europe.**

East-west trains may stop at Brunico, Dobbiaco and San Candido, connecting with trains going north-south in Bolzano to major cities in Italy and elsewhere in Europe. Zurich, Switzerland, is connected by train to the Italian Alps through a change of train at Innsbruck, Austria. Note that while restaurant cars are attached only to most international and long-distance trains, snacks and drinks are available on many others.

> ☞ **HINT: In each base village chapter we provide sample train timetables for your use in estimating the timing of your trips. However, you should ALWAYS acquire and check your own current train or bus timetables before setting out on any excursion.**

Italian words that may be useful at the train station:
arrival - *arrivi*
track - *binario*
timetable - *orario ferroviario*
platform - *piattaforma*
seat reservation - *prenotazione posti*
railroad station - *stazione ferroviaro*
baggage checkroom - *ufficio bagagli*
ticket office - *ufficio biglietto*
exit - *uscita*
departure - *partenza*
men - *uomini*
women - *donne*

Italy by Car

If you are going to be in Italy for an extended period of time, you will probably be more comfortable with a rental car. Most major car rental agencies are represented in Italy, and you can save on car rentals by making arrangements at home. Check to see whether your own auto insurance covers damage to a rental car. Your credit card company may include CDW (Collision Damage Waiver) if you charge the car rental to the credit card. You should also make sure that insurance for theft of the car is included. Confirm these facts with your credit card company and/or insurance company before making your rental car reservations.

You will need a valid driver's license from your home country plus an International Driver's License, available with two passport photos and $10 from the AAA in the United States. An International Driver's License is a viable and readily understandable additional piece of identification when traveling.

You will drive on various types of roads during your stay. Among these are *autostrade*, toll highways, and *superstrade*, free expressways. All are signed and numbered. *Raccordo* are connecting expressways, and a *strade statali* is a state highway with an "S" or "SS" number, which may be a single-lane road each way.

In Italy, you drive on the right and pass on the left, just as you do in the United States. Remember, though, that speed limits are rather different from what you may be used to: 130 kmph (80 mph) on *autostrada*, 90 kmph (55 mph) on main and local roads and 50 kmph (30 mph) in cities and towns. You should also keep in mind that many Europeans will drive over these stated speed limits. Stay to the right and use your rear view mirror often.

Road maps are sold at many Italian newstands and bookstores, and in the United States many bookstores carry "Michelin Map #988-Italy." Of course, other maps cover specific regions in more depth. An excellent road map of all of Alpine Europe, especially if you are driving from one country to another, is "Alpen/The Alps," published by Freytag & Berndt. The Automobile Club D'Italia publishes a map of "Südtirol/Dolomiten Italien." If you write to "Azienda per la Promozione Turistica del Trentino"—Via Sighele, 3, 38100 Trento, Italy—they will send you an excellent map called "Trentino Itineraries and Road Map."

The A22 *autostrada*, running north-south through the Brenner Pass, connects Austria and Germany with the Dolomites and alpine Italy. There are many exits from A22 leading east into the mountains: at Bressanone, Chiusa, Bolzano, Ora, Trento. All local roads leading into the Südtirol and/or the Dolomites are winding, and you will usually drive up and over passes through the mountains. Adjust your driving times accordingly. South and east of the Dolomites is the heavily traveled A4 (Milan to Venice) superhighway, and the A23 (east of Cortina d'Ampezzo) connects central Austria and Salzburg with Venice. Both roads have exits leading into the alps.

Horn blowing is forbidden in most towns, and the large *Zona di Silenzio* signs are your indication. A key point to remember is that Italian roadside emergency service is only a phone call away—call 116 in case of a breakdown.

Italy by Bus

Train travel in Italy is comparatively inexpensive, so Italy's bus network, while extensive, is not as comprehensive as some other European countries. However, regional bus companies are sometimes the only means, other than by car, of getting to out-of-the-way places, especially in the mountainous regions of the Italian Alps, because the gradients become too steep for train travel. Bus information is available from the local tourist offices.

Italy Up and Down

The following are important adjuncts to transportation in the Italian Alps:

Cable cars (*funivie*) - Large, enclosed cars holding up to 100 people or more and running on a fixed schedule.

Gondolas - Enclosed cars that usually hold four to eight people and which run continuously.

Chairlifts (*seggiovie*) - Sit-down or stand-up lifts that move continuously and are usually open to the weather. They can be single, double, or triple systems. When getting on a moving chairlift, stand in the designated place on the platform, holding your backpack in front of you, and sit down as the chair approaches. Once seated, reach up and pull down the front bar, putting the footrest in place. There is usually someone in attendance to help you on and off.

Funiculars - Mountain railways pulled up and down a steep incline by a cable.

Cogwheel railways or **rack and pinion railways** - These trains are drawn along by a toothed wheel which connects into the matching teeth of the rail.

Italian Discount Travel

Different Italian Rail Passes and FlexiRail Cards allow unlimited travel, over a set period, on the national rail networks of Italy, including Intercity, Eurocity and Rapido trains. These passes also permit you to make seat reservations, with no surcharge, but only while you are in Italy. (However, a supplement is required for TR 450 trains.) Validity dates **must** be marked on each pass at the first station where they are used. **All passes and railroad tickets may be bought at the Italian State Railways office, 342 Madison Avenue, New York, NY 10173.** There is a $20 fee for processing railroad tickets and a $10 fee per pass.

Italian Rail Pass	1st Class	2nd Class
8 days	$226	$152
15 days	$284	$190
21 days	$330	$220
30 days	$396	$264

Italian FlexiRail Card	1st Class	2nd Class
4 days out of 9 days	$170	$116
8 days out of 21 days	$250	$164
12 days out of 30 days	$314	$210

(all prices as of Spring 1994)

There are also "Kilometric Tickets," which permit travel for up to 20 single trips totaling no more than 3000 kilometers (1875 miles) within 60 days. If a train charges a supplement, you must pay it if you use this pass. However, the Kilometric Ticket can be used by one to five people traveling together. Like all other Italian rail passes and tickets, it is available at Italian State Railways in the United States and, unlike the other passes which must be bought outside of Italy, also can be bought in Italy at all rail stations. First-class Kilometric Tickets are about $260, with $156 being charged for second class.

The Senior Citizen's Silver Card (Carta d'Argento) can be purchased by all travelers over 60 years of age at any railway station in Italy. It allows the holder to obtain a 30% discount on the Italian State railway system and is valid for one year (except Fridays, Saturdays or Sundays from June 26 to August 14 and December 18 to 28); the cost is 10,000 lire or about $6.50.

HINT: The purchase of an Italian train pass entitles you to a 10% discount on city tours in Milan, Florence, Naples, Rome and Venice. Present the pass at any CIT (Compagnia Italiana Turismo) office.

Comfortable Inns and Hotels

Accommodations in Italy range from world-class, deluxe hotels to comfortable rooms in rural farmhouses. The quality of a hotel (*albergo*) and its prices can be judged by the number of stars awarded to it: five stars denotes deluxe; four stars, first-class; three stars, superior; two stars, standard; and one star, minimum, where the bathroom may be down the hall. For comfort, quality of food, price and convenience, we recommend three- or four-star rated hotels with half-board (breakfast and dinner) included. (Please see the "Accommodations" chapter for recommendations on specific lodgings in each base village.) If you prefer to dine at different restaurants—more expensive, but not necessarily better than dinner at your hotel on the half-board plan—try the Italian version of "bed and breakfasts," rated on the same star system as full hotels. Smaller guesthouses or *pensioni* are also available. They are less formal than hotels and usually less expensive.

Rental apartments are a viable alternative to hotels. In the Südtirol a brochure is available containing a list of apartments (*ferienwohnungen*). It is published by the Association of Private Landlords in Südtirol and is available by writing to: Regional Tourist Information Office, Verband der Privatvermeiter, Mustergasse 9, 39100 Bolzano/Bozen, Italy.

There are other, less traditional accommodations available. Farm holidays have become increasingly popular. The Südtirol Farmer's Association lists over 400 vacation farms in its directory. Write to: Südtiroler Bauernbund, Kennwort

"Urlaub auf dem Bauernhof," Brennerstrasse 7, 39100 Bolzano/Bozen, Italy. Many castles, convents and palaces in the Südtirol have been converted into hotels. You might write to the Tourist Office in each area you are interested in and ask if any are available. The Italian Automobile Club (ACI) and AGIP Oil Company have built motels (*autostelli*) in larger towns. Tourist Villages have also sprung up—these are bungalows and/or apartments built in or near popular resorts. Italy also has many camping sites, many of them in the Alps. For a list of campgrounds and information, write to: Federazione Italiana del Campeggio e de Caravanning, via Vittorio Emanuele II, I-50041 Calenzano, Firenze, Italy.

Enjoying Italian Cuisine

Eating is part of enjoying the Italian lifestyle. Sample the local cuisine in a more formal *ristorante* or a simpler, less expensive, family-run *trattoria*. Don't neglect the local *pizzeria* and *rosticceria*, less formal than the *ristorante*, usually serving crisp pizza made in wood-burning ovens along with pastas, soups, salads, etc. Breakfast, usually eaten at your hotel, may also be found at a coffee bar, where you can also buy sandwiches and snacks for later in the day. Inform the cashier of your selection and pay for it, then take the ticket to the counter and actually place the order. This is for stand-up service, table service is extra. Whichever dining experience you choose—a five-course gourmet meal or a simple country pizza—enjoy it as part of the "Italian experience."

Regional Specialties

Cuisine in Italian alpine areas can be a combination of Italian, German and Ladino specialities—depending on which village you are visiting. In the southern area of the alps, the food and wine will be distinctly Italian, but as you travel north into the Südtirol, the accent is definitely more

Tyrolean, Germanic and, in certain valleys, Ladino. Expect to find Venetian-influenced, typically Italian dishes in Cortina and Baselga and heartier, Tyrolean specialties in Selva and Merano.

Some of the more popular Südtirolean dishes are: *krapfen*, a round, fried doughnut filled with jam; *knödl suppe*, a clear soup with large bread dumplings; *weinerschnitzel*, veal cutlets, breaded and sauteed; *spaetzli*, small flour dumplings; and, of course, apple strudel—a winner in any language. Typical Italian dishes can range from *risotto con funghi*, a creamy rice with mushrooms, to *patate fritte* (french fries) to the varied pastas we all know and love. As always, Italian cheeses come in a grand variety: fresh cheeses include mascarpone, mozzarella and ricotta; mild cheeses are fontina, provolone dolce, scamorza; sharp cheeses can be asiago, gorgonzola, pecorino and provolone piccante.

One of the favorite desserts of guests at the Hotel Minerva in Merano is Tiramisù or "Italian Tipsy Cake." Peter Castelforte, director of the hotel, was able to persuade the chef to share this recipe with us:

Tiramisù Hotel Minerva
6 eggs, separated and at room temperature
100 grams granulated sugar (3½ oz.)
500 grams mascarpone cheese (17½ oz.)
1 teaspoon vanilla
lady fingers
coffee
Marsala wine

Beat the egg yolks with sugar until well mixed, add mascarpone and blend well. Whip egg whites with vanilla until they form soft peaks. Lay the lady fingers in a casserole and pour the coffee and Marsala over them, enough to soak the lady fingers without spilling into the dish. Cover with whipped yolks and whites. Repeat layers as high as they can go. Sprinkle top with unsweetened cocoa powder. Refrigerate. Serves eight to ten.

Lucia Merz, the excellent cook and owner of the Hotel Due Camini in the tiny village of Baselga di Pinè, was happy to share her recipe for traditional Green Gnocchi with *Walking Easy* readers.

Green Gnocchi Lucia
130 grams fine, unseasoned breadcrumbs (4½ oz.)
130 grams very fine (00) white flour (4½ oz.)
2 eggs
130 grams milk (4½ oz.)
1 package frozen, chopped spinach (defrosted and squeezed dry)
40 grams grated parmesan cheese (1½ oz.)
salt and pepper

Pour milk over the breadcrumbs and mix. Stir in spinach, then flour, and mix with hands to consistency of chewing gum (add a touch more flour if necessary). Have a large pot of water boiling with a little salt. Wet a teaspoon with the boiling water and use it to scoop a teaspoon of dough. Put the spoonful of dough in the boiling water, and repeat the process until all dough is used. When the gnocchi come to the top they are ready. Scoop out with slotted spoon and serve with melted butter and the grated cheese. Serves four.

An Italian Food Primer
amaretti - crunchy, sweet, almond macaroons
antipasti - various appetizers
bistecca alla fiorentina - steak with olive oil, pepper, lemon, salt
braciola - pork chops
bresaola - air-dried beef
bruschetta - toasted bread with butter, garlic and tomatoes
cannelloni - stuffed crepes baked in a white sauce
cappelletti - small ravioli stuffed with meat or cheese
carciofi - artichokes
fagioli - white beans
fegato alla veneziana - calves' liver with salt, pepper and onions
foccacia - bread spread with tomato sauce, garlic, basil, olive oil
fritto misto - deep-fried fresh fish

fusilli - spiral-shaped pasta
gelato - ice cream
gnocchi - potato dumplings
granita - flavored ice, usually lemon or coffee
insalata di frutti di mare - seafood salad
osso buco - veal knuckle simmered until tender
panne - heavy cream
pesto - basil green sauce with cheese, garlic and pine nuts
piccata al marsala - scallops of veal in a marsala wine sauce
pizzaiola - steak covered with tomato sauce
polenta - cornmeal
pollo alla cacciatore - chicken with tomatoes, mushrooms, wine
ragù - meat sauce
rigatoni - large, ridged macaroni
risotto - various creamy rice dishes
saltimbocca - veal scalop layered with prosciutto
scaloppine - thin slices of sauteed veal
semifreddo - frozen dessert, usually ice cream and cake
sogliola - sole
spiedino - pieces of grilled meat
tiramisu - rich, creamy cheese and rum-soaked sponge cake
tonno - tuna
tortellini - rings of dough stuffed with ground meat or cheese

Beverages

Wine: The production of wine is influenced by the proximity of the Südtirol to Austria. There are almost two dozen varieties bottled, from the pale yellow or green Riesling, Pinot Bianco and Terlano, and the straw-yellow Traminer, to a ruby-red Santa Magdalena. The white Riesling and Gewürztraminer are dry, crisp and aromatic. The southern end of the Italian Alps or Trentino area produces a red Cabernet and Teraldo Rotaliano, similar to Beaujolais.

For those *Easy Walkers* who might enjoy visiting a winery: Terlan, near Merano, is well-known for its Chardonnay and Sauvignon. Visit the Terlan Wine Cellar Cooperative (Kellereigenossenschaft Terlan) on Silberleitenweg for a taste

of young white wine. Also near Merano, the well-known An-
drian Wine Cellar Cooperative (Kellereigenossenschaft An-
drian) is situated on the southern slopes of the Etsch Valley.
The Eisack Valley Wine Cellar Cooperative (Eisacktaler Kellereigenossenschaft) in Chiusa/Klausen is located next to the
Neustift Monastery cellars near Bressanone/Brixen, and is
the most important wine cellar co-op in the Eisack/Isarco
Valley. In Bolzano/Bozen, stop in at the St. Magdalena Wine
Cellar Cooperative (Kellereigenossenschaft St. Magdalena)
on Brennerstrasse 15, to sample a familiar South Tyrol wine
at its source.

☞ **HINT: Red=***rosso***, white=***bianco***, rosé=***rosato***, dry=**
secco **or** ***asciutto***, **sweet=***dolce***, and bubbly=***spumanti***.

Beer: Beer brewed in Italy is usually lighter than German
beer, and many companies with familiar German names
brew their beer specially formulated in Italy to the Italian
taste. When in Italy you should specify Italian beer or you
will be served higher-cost imported beer.

Liqueur: You can order almond-flavored Amaretto, herb-
flavored Galliano or Strega, cherry-flavored Maraschino, or
anise-flavored Sambucca traditionally served with coffee
beans in the glass. Campari is the most famous aperitif,
bright red and bitter from its herbs, usually served with ice
and club soda. Grappa has a high alcohol content and is
made after the wine has been pressed. Drunk before or after
dinner, it is considered to be an acquired taste.

Coffee: Drinking coffee is an important part of Italian life.
Italians normally drink *espresso,* very strong, black coffee,
served in small cups. Strong coffee with foaming hot milk
and a sprinkling of grated chocolate is *cappuccino. Caffè
latte* is a large cup of coffee with hot milk, usually drunk at
breakfast. A double measure of *espresso* is called *caffè*

doppio. Extra-strong coffee is *caffè ristretto*, while a weak black coffee is *caffè alto* or *lungo*. *Caffè macchiato* is black coffee with a dash of milk, while *latte macchiato* is the opposite, a glass of milk with a dash of coffee. *Caffè montata* is coffee with whipped cream, and *caffè corretto* is served with some brandy or *grappa* in it.

Mineral Water: Called *acqua minerale*, it comes carbonated (*frizzante* or *gassata*) or without bubbles (*naturale*).

Where to Eat and Drink

Hotels: Three- and four-star Italian hotels in the alps usually offer a buffet breakfast (more lavish in the Südtirol), and a four-course meal for dinner, if you take half-board. Hotel food in Italy is uniformly excellent, and *Easy Walkers* can take advantage of lower costs by booking with dinner. The typical breakfast consists of juice, rolls, bread, butter and jam, cold cereal, perhaps cold meat and cheese, yoghurt, and a hot beverage. Dinner can consist of a first course or *primo piatto* of pasta or soup, a second course or *secondi piatti* with meat, fish or poultry and potatoes, followed by salad, and dessert (*dolci*) or fruit (*frutta*). Unlike France, the cheese course is usually eliminated in the Italian Alps unless you are staying in a four- or five-star hotel. Most diners prefer to take their after-dinner coffee later at an outdoor café or in the hotel sitting room.

Restaurants: If you decide not to eat at your hotel, notify the hotel desk at least 24 hours in advance. Check out the restaurant's *menu turistico*, usually including three courses and often 1/4 liter of wine or mineral water, as well as bread, cover charge and tip (although you should always leave a small extra tip). The fixed price *prezzo fisso* menu is probably lower in price than the tourist menu, but it doesn't include wine, bread, cover charge and tip—you'll be billed for all of these—and it usually isn't as good a buy as the *menu turistico*.

> ☞ **HINT: A bread and cover charge (*pane e caperto*) are added in most Italian restaurants—1000 to 2000 lire ($.60 to $1.20) per person. The tip (*servizio*) is included in the bill, but since it is 10% to 15%, it is customary to leave something extra if the service was satisfactory.**

In Italy the word "bar" has a different meaning than it does in America or Britain. The average bar is popular at breakfast, most often serving *cappuccino* or *caffè* to their customers with an accompaniment of sugared doughnuts (*bombolini*), croissants and brioches. At lunch, bars usually offer rolls (*panini*) with cold ham, cheese or salami. The least expensive way to drink at a bar is to pay for what you want at the cashier, who will give you a receipt. Hand the receipt to the barman, stating what you've paid for, and drink your coffee standing at the bar. Waiter service will cost more, and remember that once you've purchased your drink, you cannot bring it to a table.

Picknicking: When planning a day of walking, we recommend taking a picnic lunch in your backpack. The bakery (*panificio*) will astound you with its choice of bread and rolls, and you can select a local cheese and/or sliced cooked meat in the grocery (*drogheria*). Fresh fruit completes a healthy and inexpensive meal. Mustard can be bought in reusable squeeze tubes. Mineral water, juice and soda are available in plastic bottles or cans.

Dressing for the Trail—From Boots to Backpack

Walking Easy clothing ideally should be lightweight and layerable. All clothing is not suitable for all types of walking—climate, altitude and time of day during the alpine hiking season are points to consider. *Easy Walkers* must make a decision each day, taking the above factors into consideration. It is not necessary to bring a dress, skirt, sport jacket, stockings, dress shoes or pocketbook on this walking vacation. However, a classic mix of slacks layered with shirts and sweaters is essential and can take you to dinner or sightseeing. In fact, the mix and match possibilities of two pair of slacks, two knit turtleneck shirts, two long-sleeved shirts and two sweaters create inumerable combinations and have taken the authors through two months of alpine evenings!

Shoes: The most important item for a satisfactory *Walking Easy* experience is a good pair of broken-in, medium-weight hiking boots, preferably waterproof. These can be above or below the ankle, with the higher ones providing more support on rocky or steep trails. Do **not** wear sneakers or sneakers that look like hiking boots, as they do not provide the support and traction needed. Remember, $60 hiking boots do not have the same level of construction as $120 boots—the durability, waterproofing, foot stability and overall quality are not the same in a less expensive shoe. All boots will probably feel good when the trail is level and smooth, but remember the ascents, descents, stones and rain!

Socks: Experts tell us that socks worn closest to the skin should **not** be made of cotton. Cotton absorbs perspiration and holds it, possibly producing friction, leading to blisters. A lightweight undersock made of a "hydrophobic" or water-hating synthetic will wick sweat away from your feet and keep them drier. Whether you prefer to wear one or two pair of socks, when purchasing hiking boots, make sure to wear the type of socks you will wear on the trail.

Outerwear: An insulated jacket or vest is essential for walking and sightseeing over 8000 ft. (2500 m). These jackets are easily put into backpacks when not needed and can be carried on to the plane. Rain protection is best provided by a good quality, waterproof poncho with a snap-down back to fit over a backpack (available from L.L. Bean), or a waterproof jacket. Don't let a drizzle or light rain cancel your walking plans.

Hats: A hat with a brim provides protection from sun as well as rain and should always be worn.

Pants: Many alpine walkers wear jeans—an acceptable choice if they are not skin-tight, do not restrict movement and are not too warm in hot weather. Cotton chinos are also satisfactory, and in summer, walking shorts should be considered. However, our favorite walking apparel in any type of climate is alpine hiking knickers. They fasten below the knee and are worn with high socks which protect the legs from bushes and brambles, cold temperatures and insects, but can be rolled down in warmer weather. These knickers, for both men and women, are comfortable for all types of walking, and you'll see them being worn on trails throughout Europe. They can be purchased in most sporting goods stores in the Italian Alps.

Sweaters: A medium-weight sweater is essential for cool evenings in the mountains, even in summer.

Sweatshirts: Medium-weight sweatshirts can be layered over short- or long-sleeved knit shirts for hiking.

Shirts: While many prefer 100% natural fibers for comfort, a cotton/polyster blend can be used for ease of laundering, as it will dry overnight. Short-sleeved knit shirts, along with long-sleeved knits and turtlenecks, are essential for layering under sweaters and sweatshirts, for both day and evening.

Backpack: Each *Easy Walker* should carry a lightweight nylon backpack with wide, extra-heavy, adjustable foam shoulder straps. Roomy, outside zipper compartments (three to four if possible), are necessary to organize day-backpacking essentials, i.e., camera equipment, lunch, water, sunscreen, binoculars, emergency roll of toilet tissue, rain gear, jacket or sweater, etc.

Waist or Fanny Pack: Use a well-made, comfortable waist pack to carry money, traveler's checks, passport, etc. No pocketbook is necessary on a walking vacation. Hands should be left free for a walking stick and/or camera.

Walking Stick: We recommend a walking cane or walking stick with a pointed, metal tip for **all** *Easy Walkers*. These sticks are an indispensible aid to balance when walking downhill or on rocky terrain. They come in many sizes and styles and can usually be purchased at a village sporting goods store. The newest walking stick innovation looks like a telescoping aluminum ski pole. It fits into your backpack when not in use. We think this item is a "must."

Luggage Carrier: A small, fold-up luggage carrier may be necessary to help transport luggage from the train, bus or car to the hotel, and back again. However, luggage with built-in wheels is easier to handle.

Pack Light and Right

Keep luggage small, lightweight and expandable, even when using a luggage carrier.

1. Wear your hiking boots for overseas and inter-city travel—they can be heavy and bulky to carry or pack. Remove them on the plane, perhaps changing to a pair of lightweight slippers you have put into your backpack.

2. On the plane, wear comfortable slacks, knit shirt and an unlined jacket, along with your waist pack and hiking boots. A lightweight warm-up suit can be a good alterna-

tive—the jacket can be worn when it is too warm for your insulated jacket or vest.

3. Every *Easy Walker* should have a lightweight backpack to use as his/her carry-on luggague. When traveling, your backpack should include:

a) All drugs and toiletries, with prescriptions in a separate zippered pouch for easy accessibility.

b) For the plane, one change of socks, underwear and knit shirt, rolled into a plastic bag—just in case.

c) Slippers for the plane and later bedroom use.

d) Waterproof outerwear, always left in the bottom of your backpack.

e) Reading material for the plane or train.

f) Roll of toilet paper in a plastic bag.

g) Insulated jacket or vest (you might carry this).

h) Incidentals such as: binoculars, compass, whistle, pedometer, tiny flashlight, pocket knife, plastic bags, sewing kit, sunglasses, travel alarm clock, small address book or pre-printed labels, small packs of tissues and "handi-wipes," and of course, your *Walking Easy in the Italian Alps* guidebook.

i) Photographic equipment, unless carried separately.

EASY WALKERS' UNISEX PACKING CHECKLIST

_____ 6 pr. underwear
_____ 3 bras
_____ 7 pr. socks (3 long hiking, 2 undersocks, 2 evening)
_____ 2 pr. shoes (1 hiking, 1 for evening)
_____ 1 pr. lightweight slippers
_____ 1 belt
_____ 1 pajamas/nightgown
_____ 1 lightweight robe (optional)
_____ 1 bathing suit (optional)
_____ 2 sweaters
_____ 2 sweatshirts
_____ 1 jacket or vest, down or insulated
_____ 2 pr. hiking pants or knickers
_____ 2 pr. walking shorts (depending on month)
_____ 2 pr. casual slacks for evening

_____ 2 shirts or blouses, long-sleeved
_____ 4 knit shirts, short-sleeved
_____ 2 knit shirts, long-sleeved turtleneck
_____ 1 hat
_____ 1 rain outfit (poncho)
_____ 1 walking stick
_____ 1 waistpack

 HINT: Small towns may not have laundry facilities or hotel valet service, and if you wash underwear, socks and knit shirts each night before dinner, you will always be ahead—very important on trips longer than two weeks. Remember that clothes can take two days to dry if they are 100% cotton. Shirts or underwear containing poly/cotton will dry overnight.

For Your Information—From Telephones to Tipping

Credit Cards: Most retail stores accept credit cards, as do most hotels and restaurants. Mountain inns or _rifugios_ do not. Find out if your hotels accept credit cards before leaving home, otherwise take enough American traveler's checks to cover your hotel bills, plus all other non-chargeable expenses. Master Card and Visa are widely accepted in Italian stores, along with American Express and Diners Club. A store or hotel listing "Eurocard" or "Access" usually accepts Master Card. Charging can work in your favor because of the favorable rate of exchange large companies receive.

 HINT: Keep a record of charge card numbers and telephone numbers for reporting a lost or stolen card in a separate place from where you keep your credit cards.

Customs: Returning from Italy to the United States, American citizens are allowed to bring $400 worth of duty-free merchandise if they've been outside the country for at least

48 hours and not claimed exemptions in the previous 30 days. A flat rate of 10% is assessed for items from $400 to $1400. Gifts up to a total of $50 per day can be mailed home without declaring them on the customs form—don't send alcohol, tobacco or perfume worth more than $5, however. Keep all receipts of purchase in one place, easily retrievable (we use a small, zip-lock plastic bag), for customs purposes.

Electricity: In Italy, electricity can be 42- to 50-cycle, alternating current with 220 voltage. Bring a convertor to reduce the voltage from 220 to 110 volts and an adaptor to change the U.S. flat prongs to Italy's round-pronged plugs.

Embassies and Consulates:

US Embassy:	Via Vittorio Veneto 19 A, Rome; tel:06/46741.
US Consulates:	Lungarno Amerigo Vespucci 46, Florence; tel:055/2398276.
	Largo Donegani 1, Milan; tel:02/29001841.
	Piazza Protello 6, Genoa; tel:010/282741

Emergency Telephone Numbers: Police, fire or ambulance, 113; car breakdown, 116.

Gasoline: Gasoline is a very expensive proposition in Italy (you cannot use American gasoline credit cards even though the sign may read "Esso," etc.). If you are renting a car it may pay to buy gasoline discount coupons in a package offering free breakdown service and free highway toll vouchers. This package **must** be paid for outside Italy at European Auto Clubs, Italian Government Tourist Offices (ENIT) in Europe, or their offices at busy Italian border crossings. To buy these vouchers you must be a tourist driving a non-diesel car with a non-Italian registration. These "Tourist Incentive Packages" save about 15% on gas prices. On the *autostrade*, gas stations are open 24 hours a day, but on regular roads they probably close between noon and 2:00 pm, after 7:00 pm and are not open on Sundays or holidays.

When traveling the alpine roads it doesn't hurt to be on the safe side and "top off" when the tank registers half-full.

> ☞ **HINT: Check to make sure the attendant has pushed the pump back to zero before he fills your car or you'll be paying double, for your gas and the person before you, who already paid!**

Government: Italy is a Parliamentary Republic, headed by a President elected for seven years, with two Houses of Parliament—the Chamber of Deputies and the Senate. The country is divided into 20 regions for administrative purposes and 94 provinces. Among others, the Trentino/Alto Adige/Südtirol (encompassing the Dolomites), is under special statute and has some administrative autonomy. This is the area formerly belonging to Austria.

Health: A list of English-speaking doctors in Italy is available from the International Association for Medical Assistance to Travelers (AMAT) at 716-754-4883. Those with chronic illnesses such as diabetes or a heart condition are advised wear a "Medic Alert Identification Tag." In the United States call 800-432-5378 for information. They also provide a 24-hour hotline a foreign doctor can call to access your medical records. U.S. Travelers on Medicare should check their Medicare supplement for foreign coverage.

> ☞ **HINT: Remember that an increased intake of wine and olive oil, which many Americans do not consume in great quantity at home, can have a laxative effect.**

Holidays: Banks, offices, stores, museums, and even many gas stations are closed on national holidays:

Jan. 1	New Year's Day
Jan. 6	Epiphany
(varies)	Easter Sunday & Monday
Apr. 25	Liberation Day
May 1	Labor Day

Aug. 15	Assumption of the Virgin (Ferragosto)
Nov. 1	All Saints Day
Dec. 8	Feast of the Immaculate Conception
Dec. 25	Christmas
Dec. 26	Santo Stefano

Insurance: Before purchasing additional insurance of any kind, *Easy Walkers* should review their existing policies and determine whether the coverage is adequate for overseas travel. Homeowner policies may cover luggage, theft and/or plane tickets, and your local insurance agent or credit card company may cover your automotive insurance needs while traveling. Contact your travel agent for companies offering the following types of travel insurance:

1) Trip cancellation and interruption - provides a refund if a trip must be cancelled or interrupted while in progress.

2) Personal accident and sickness - covers illness, injury or death.

3) Default and/or bankruptcy - provides coverage in case the airline, etc. defaults or goes bankrupt.

4) Baggage and personal effects - protects your luggage and contents against damage or theft.

5) Automobile insurance - provides collision, theft, property damage and personal liability protection.

> ☞ **HINT: If you are driving in Europe you will need an international insurance certificate, called a green card. Your car rental or lease agency MUST give you one before you take the car to begin your trip.**

Language: Italian is the official language of Italy, with many dialects spoken in different regions. In the Südtirol, Italian and German are both official languages, and town names are listed both ways, i.e., Selva/Wolkenstein, etc. In many of the Dolomite valleys of this mountainous region, however, Ladin is spoken along with Italian and German. It is an unusual language, formed when Roman soldiers moved into Dolomite valleys and their Latin blended with the language of the native mountain population. This ancient language is preserved today in the Dolomites, the Friuli region of Italy, and the Swiss Engadine. About 40,000 people in the valleys of Gardena, di Fassa, Badia and Livinallongo speak the language—and two of the *Easy Walking* base villages of Selva and Vigo di Fassa are excellent examples of rural villages preserving their Ladin heritage.

Following are translations of some Italian words found on directional signs and hiking maps:

alpe - upland meadow
alto - high
baita - mountain hut
bosco - forest
canalone - gully
cengia - ledge
chiuso - closed
cima - summit
col, colle - hill
destra - right
diritto - straight ahead
dislivello - varied altitude
esposto - exposed
est - east
fiume - river
forcella - small pass
ghicciaio - glacier
giu - down
in salita - uphill
joch - pass (German)
lontano - far
montagna - mountain
nebbia - fog
nord - north

occidentale - western
orientale - eastern
ovest - west
passeggiata - walk
passo - pass
percorso - path
pericolo - danger
piano - level
piz - summit
ponte - bridge
ripido - steep
scendere - to go down
sentiero - trail
sinistra - left
skilift - t-bar lift
strada - road
sud - south
tempo - weather
traversata - crossing
val, valle - valley
vento - wind
via - way, route
vietato - not permitted

Laundry: Look in the classified telephone directory under *lavanderie*, laundry, or *tintorie*, cleaning and pressing.

Mail: In addition to the Post Office, stamps are also sold in tobacco stores (*tabacci*) with blue signs reading "valori e bollati." Local Post Offices are usually open Monday to Friday from 8:00 am to 1:00 pm. Do send all mail to and from Italy by air for faster response—it may still take a few weeks to arrive! Airmail postcards to the U.S. are 1100 lire.

To have mail held for someone to pick up at a local Italian post office, the envelope must have a return name and address as well as the recipient's name, the name of their town and its postal code. For example:

Mr. Gordo Baier
c/o Ufficio Postale Central
Fermo Posta
32043, Cortina d'Ampezzo
Italy

Medications: If you are using a prescription drug, bring more than an adequate supply in case you are delayed returning home, plus a prescription for the medication using its generic name in case a local doctor must write a new one. Carry over-the-counter medication to relieve diarrhea, sunburn, constipation, indigestion, colds and allergies, cuts and bruises, as well as a small first aid kit. Whether traveling overseas or between villages, always carry all medications in your backpack in case there is a problem with your luggage.

If you wear glasses, carry a spare pair and a copy of your prescription.

Measurements: Italy operates on the metric system. To convert kilometers to miles, multiply the number of kilometers by .62; to convert meters to feet, multiply the number of meters by 3.281; to convert liters to U.S. gallons, multiply the number of liters by .26; to convert kilograms to pounds, multiply the kilograms by 2.2; to convert Celsius to Fahrenheit degrees, multiply Celsius degrees by 9, divide by 5, and add 32.

Money: The basic unit of Italian currency is the lira or (plural) lire. Coins are issued in denominations of 10, 20, 50, 100, 500 and 1000 lire; bills in 1000, 2000, 5000, 10,000, 100,000 and 500,000 lire. Cash and traveler's checks can be exchanged for local currency at any bank or money exchange counter, with a small commission added to the official exchange rate. Banks are closed Saturdays and Sundays and are usually open Monday to Friday from 8:00 am to 1:00 pm and 2:45 to 4:00 pm. Money also can be changed at all airports and railroad stations if banks are closed, just look for the *Ufficio di Cambio* sign; they often have the best deals and the easiest, quickest service.

The exchange rate fluctuates daily, but to convert Italian lire into U.S. dollars, multiply the number of lire by the exchange rate. For example, if your hotel room costs 200,000 lire per day and the exchange rate is 1 lira = .0006 $U.S., multiply 200,000 by .0006—your hotel room will cost $120 American money.

☞ **HINT: Not all banks and agencies use the same exchange rate and commission charge. Shop around for the best deal.**

Museums: Always check local museum openings and closings—hours and days of closing vary with the season. Travelers over 60 years of age are entitled to free admission to state museums and many other museums. Ask at the ticket office and use your passport for proof of age.

Newspapers: In many small towns in Italy, a newsstand can usually be found that sells the *International Herald Tribune* or *USA Today*, published in English Monday through Saturday. Newsstands or kiosks can also be found at railroad stations. In smaller villages, these newspapers may arrive one day late, i.e., the Thursday paper is sold on Friday.

Passport: A passport valid past your time of return is necessary to stay in Italy for a vacation of up to 90 days. Before leaving the United States, photocopy the information on your first two passport pages, in case it is lost. Since you'll be carrying the original passport in your waist pack, put the copy in another place.

Restrooms: Designated with the general sign "W.C." for water closet and *donne* for women and *uomini* for men. Less distinguishable, so be careful, is *signori* for men and *signore* for women!

Shopping Hours: Most store hours in Italy are Monday to Friday from 9:00 am to 1:00 pm and 3:30 to 7:00 or 7:30 pm. Some are open a half day on Saturday but are usually closed on Sunday, except in heavily traveled tourist areas. Check the store hours in each area you visit.

Telephone: A public phone requires coins, tokens (*gettone*) or a prepaid calling card (*scheda*); either can be bought at tobacco shops or Telefoni offices. To use the now-common *scheda*, which can be bought for 5000 or 10,000 lire:
1) Insert card as indicated by the arrow.
2) Value will be visible in the little window.
3) Dial the number.
4) After completing the call, hang-up.
5) Card will be returned.
6) Use it again until its value runs out.

   To use a coin or token (*gettone*):
1) Deposit a 200 lire coin or token in the slot.
2) Dial the number.
3) Release the token or coin after your party has answered.

   For local credit card calls:
1) Dial 170.
2) An ITALCABLE English-speaking operator will place the call.

   For international credit card calls:
1) Dial 001 for the United States + area code + number calling.

   ☞ **HINT: In Italy, the number for the AT&T operator is 172-1011, for MCI, 172-1022, and Sprint, 172-1877.**

Time: Italy is in the Middle European Time Zone, six hours ahead of Eastern Standard Time in the United States. They observe Daylight Savings Time between May and September—check for the exact dates. Italy uses European time, based on the 24-hour clock, and all timetables are written in this manner. For example, 13:10 is 1:10 pm in the United States, and 18:40 is 6:40 pm.

Tipping or *Mancia*: Hotels build in a service charge of 15 to 19% to the bill; restaurants add 15% to the bill. However, you may tip the chambermaid 1000 lire per day or 5000 lire per week, a doorman 1000 lire for calling a cab, a porter or bellboy 2000 lire a bag, and the concierge 3000 lire a day plus extra for extra services. In restaurants, an additional tip is expected—from small change to another 10%. In every restaurant operated by Italians there is a cover charge of 1000 to 3000 lire per person for bread (*pane e coperto*), even if you don't want bread! Remember, this does not take the place of an extra tip. In cafés and bars, tip 15% of the bill if the tip is not included. Taxi drivers expect a 15% tip. Tipping seems to be a way of life in Italy—even at a stand-up coffee bar a 100-lire tip (about 6 1/2 cents!) is expected.

Tourist Information Offices: These offices, designated in Italy by a large "i," are a valuable friend to the hiker. They are usually found on the main street of even the smallest village and near or in the railroad station in larger towns. The personnel are friendly, usually multilingual, and can help with everything from hotel reservations to local hiking maps. When preparing for your trip, write to the tourist offices (*Azienda di Soggiorno*) in the towns you plan to visit and ask them to send information on hotels, walking and sight-seeing activities.

The Italian National Tourist Offices can provide brochures on accommodations, maps, rail passes, sightseeing and general information about every aspect of a vacation in Italy. Write to them at:

630 Fifth Ave., #1565, New York, NY 10111; tel: 212-245-4822
500 North Michigan Ave., Chicago, IL 60611; tel: 312-644-0990
360 Post St., #801, San Francisco, CA 94108; tel: 415-392-6206

Traveler's Checks: Traveler's checks are not available in Italian lire. Buy American traveler's checks and carry no more than $200 U.S. in cash. Traveler's checks may receive a better exchange rate than cash when they are converted to lire in Italy. American traveler's checks such as American Express, Citicorp, MasterCard International/Thomas Cook International and Barclays Bank/Bank of America are readily converted at banks and money exchanges.

VAT or IVA: In Italy a "value added tax" averaging 19% is imposed on all consumer goods and services. To obtain a refund you must spend at least 525,000 lire (about $325) on one item. To help you through the complicated refund process, European Tax-free Shopping (ETS) service is available in over 70,000 stores throughout Europe. They will assist you in the paperwork for a fee of 15 to 20% of the VAT amount to be returned. Send a stamped, self-addressed envelope to: European Tax-free Shopping, 111 W. Monroe St., Suite 2100E, Chicago, IL 60603; tel: 312-346-9126, for a list of participating stores and procedures to follow. To claim an Italian IVA refund yourself, you should:

1) At the time of purchase, take a receipt from the seller.

2) At the point you leave Italy (airport, border stop, etc.), find the Italian Customs agent.

3) Show him/her the item and receipt.

4) He will stamp the vendor's receipt.

5) When you get home, photocopy the receipt and mail the original, stamped receipt back to the original vendor.

6) The vendor will send you a refund of the VAT tax.

Water: Most visitors use bottled mineral water for drinking purposes. When out walking, always carry a large bottle of water in your backpack and stop frequently for a drink.

Rules of the Road

* Plan your route by checking *Walking Easy in the Italian Alps* and your local hiking map before beginning each walk.

* Ask about local weather conditions at your hotel and adjust the day's activities accordingly.

* Always tell someone about your planned route, either a friend or the hotel staff.

* Take your time, especially at higher altitudes—alpine walking is not a race. Walking at a slow, steady pace also provides more time for enjoyment of the scenery.

* Never leave the marked trail.

* Turning back is not a disgrace—if you feel the trail is too difficult or the weather looks threatening, return on the same path or check public transportation in the area.

* Make sure your hiking shoes are in good shape and that you pack the proper equipment, plus food and water, in your backpack.

* In case of accident, stay calm and send for help. If this is not possible, use the standard alpine emergency signal: once every ten seconds call, whistle, wave clothing, signal with mirror or flashlight, for one second. Having sent six signals, spaced evenly within one minute, pause for one minute, then repeat until your signal has been answered. Confirmation is a signal every 20 seconds (three times per minute).

* Don't litter. Take out what you bring in and carry plastic bags in your backpack for this purpose.

* Close any gate you've opened—you don't want to be responsible for livestock straying.

* The mountains are for everyone's enjoyment—appreciate the beauty of the wildflowers, but don't pick them.

The purpose of any walking trip is to have fun. So take a hike...you can do it!

Explanation of Symbols

All walks can be accomplished by a recreational walker of any age, in good health. The following *Walking Easy* symbols are displayed at the beginning of each walk:

Gentle lower-level walks with few ascents and descents, usually through valleys, around lakes and along rivers on wide paths.

Comfortable ascents and descents over mixed terrain; trails can be narrower.

More challenging ascents and descents, on narrow paths with some rocky areas on parts of the trail.

Trail maps are visual indications of the walking route and are **not** drawn to scale!

SELVA/WOLKENSTEIN

The picturesque *Walking Easy* base village of
Selva/Wolkenstein is nestled in a sunny green meadow in
the Val Gardena (Gardena Valley) between the majestic
peaks and imposing rock formations of the "pale mountains"
or Dolomites. The rocky giants of Stevia, Pizes da Cir, Sella
and Sassolungo tower above Selva, while the two forest
areas of Dantercepies and Ciampinoi act as buffer zones
between village, meadow and mountain.

The earliest road through this enchanting valley was built
in 1856, and it brought geologists, biologists and mountain-
eers, soon followed by tourists and hikers. The valley was
part of Austria at the time, but in 1919 its province was
separated from Austria and incorporated into Italy, the reason for the double and sometimes triple town names and
culture—Italian, German and Ladino. Many of the place
names, including those of rivers and mountains, provide evidence that the entire Dolomite area supported settlements
well before the time of Christ.

However, about 15 B.C., the various peoples of the Central Alps, all speaking different languages and belonging to
different races, were forcibly united into a new Roman province called Rhaetia. There was a period of colonization by
Rome, with an influx of soldiers, merchants, officials and
new settlers who introduced Latin into the area. This language was modified by the original inhabitants who wove it
into their existing language structure, and thus the Ladin language of the Val Gardena evolved over many centuries. Today's Ladins speak this Rhaeto-Roman dialect, one of the

world's oldest languages, based on Latin with traces of Catalonian, Provençal and French, and the old expressions are kept alive in local legends and songs. In Selva/Wolkenstein, population 2300, a large percentage of the local population still speak Ladino, and children study the language in school, along with Italian and German.

Some examples of Ladino that may be fun to use during your stay in the Gardena Valley:

hot; cold - *ciaut*; *frëit*
breakfast; lunch; supper - *l gustè*; *la marënda*; *la cëina*
good morning; good evening - *bon di*; *bona sëira*
the room - *la majon*
the skilift - *la furnadoia*
the mountain - *l crëp*
thank you - *ldie tl pai*
How are you? - *Co vala pa?*
Well, thank you. - *Bona, ldie tl pai.*
A glass of wine, please. - *N got de vin, ldie tl pai.*
A glass of beer, please. - *N pier, ldie tl pai.*

Ladino pronunciation hints:

"C" before "i" and "e" and at the end of a word is like "ch."
"C" before "a," "o" and "u" is like the "c" in cow.
"Ch" is like the "c" in cow.
"E" is like the "a" in care.
"G" is like the "g" in get, except before "e" when it is like the "g" in gentle.
"Gh" before "i" and "e" is like like the "g" in get.
"J" is pronounced as the French "j" in journal (like "zh").

The beautiful Val Gardena includes the neighboring villages of Selva/Wolkenstein, S. Cristina and the more cosmopolitan Ortesei/St. Ulrich. Selva at 5128 ft. (1563 m.) at one end of the valley is the entrance into the tranquil, unspoiled glacial Vallunga/Langental valley and the high, twisting Sella and Gardena passes.

Two major gondola lifts operate during the summer in Selva, both used during *Easy Walker* excursions and hikes.

The Ciampinoi gondola will take you to the start of a hike to Sassolungo and Passo Sella, with a return through the valley to Plan de Gralba and Selva. The Dantercepies lift takes walkers up for a hike to Passo Gardena and the meadows and forests surrounding Selva.

Charming Santa Cristina, with its old town center and many farms situated on the steep sides of Mont Pic, is between Selva and Ortesei, and has two major summer lifts taking thousands of day-hikers to the impressive plateau Col Raiser on one side of the valley, and to Monte Pano on the other side. Signed valley walking paths connect Selva and Santa Cristina to Ortesei, the major commercial and cultural center of the Val Gardena, with its beautiful 17th-century church, carefully maintained walking street, colorfully decorated buildings, fascinating shops filled with local handcrafts, and wood-carving workshops. Ortesei lifts include a cable car which rises to the Alpe di Siusi at 6562 ft. (2005 m.), a particularly beautiful plateau and Europe's largest alp. A double lift rises to 8203 ft. (2500 m.), to the lookout and Ristorante Seceda, for viewing of the Dolomites to the north and east.

The first inhabitants of the Gardena valley were poor mountain farmers, and at the beginning of the 17th century when the art of wood-carving developed, it was a turning point in their harsh lives. The first wood-carving school in the Val Gardena was set up in Ortesei in 1872. Creative wood-carving, all by hand, continues to be a major commercial and cultural force in the valley, with skills handed down from father to son over generations; in August the valley celebrates this art form with public exhibitions of artists converting inanimate, massive blocks of wood into dramatic, highly personal works of art.

Tourist Offices in the Val Gardena are particularly efficient, offering colorful English-language brochures, a source of useful walking and cultural information in and around the region. At the Selva Tourist Office ask for the English-version "Guide to Selva—Summer." In Ortesei ask for the English-language "Holiday Guide."

> ☞ **HINT: Try to visit the Val Gardena during the months of July and September—August can be hectic, the countryside filled with happy Italian families.**

The entire valley gears up for walkers from all over Europe, offering frequent local bus service, well-maintained and well-marked trails, unparallelled views of the surrounding Dolomites, and a large variety of three- and four-star hotels providing quality accommodations at all levels. The inhabitants of the Gardena Valley try to maintain their ancient language, their beautiful old costumes, and their traditional alpine food such as doughnuts (*crafuncins da ula vërda*) and barley soup with smoked pork and dumplings (*panicia cun cërn sfumiëda y bales*). The area's inhabitants still tell ancient stories of a land of mythical creatures—dwarfs, gnomes, elves, earth-shattering giants and princes who created edelweiss from moonbeams. Enjoy the enchanting atmosphere of Selva and the Val Gardena.

Transportation to Selva/Wolkenstein

By Plane: The international airport at Munich is 186 miles (300 km) from Selva, as is the airport in Milan. The Venice airport is 155 miles (250 km) from Selva, but always requires a change of plane if flying from the United States. There are train and bus connections through Bolzano/Bozen from all airports. Car rentals are available at all airports.

By Train: The nearest train station to Selva is at Bolzano. You can transfer to the "SAD" (Servizi Autobus Dolomiti/Südtiroler Autobus Dienst) bus, or rent a car for the trip to Selva.

By Bus: There is local "SAD" bus service from Bolzano, Bressanone and Chiusa to Selva.

Sample Bus Timetable:

Dep. Bolzano	3:10 pm	4:15 pm
Arr. Selva	4:57 pm	5:37 pm

By Car: From the north, take *autostrada* A22 and exit at Chiusa/Klausen. Follow the signs to 242 east and the Val Gardena. You will pass through Ortesei/St. Ulrich and Santa Cristina before arriving in Selva.

From the south, take the *autostrada* A22 and exit at Waidbruck/Ponte Gardena, taking 242 east into Selva.

From the east and Cortina d'Ampezzo, use 48 west from Cortina over Passo Falzarego and Passo Pordoi, picking up 242 west to Selva over the Passo Sella. Major roads into the area are the Passo Gardena/Grödner Joch at 6959 ft. (2121 m.), Passo Sella/Sellajoch at 7363 ft. (2244 m.) and Passo Pordoi at 7510 ft. (2289 m.).

Activities in Selva/Wolkenstein

This section lists activities available in Selva when additions or alternatives to walking are desired. The Tourist Office is located on the main street, via Meisules, and is open Monday to Saturday from 8:00 am to noon and 3:00 pm to 5:30 pm, Sundays from 9:00 am to noon, and in the holiday season of August also from 4:00 to 6:00 pm; tel: 795122. This busy and helpful "i" can provide hiking maps, brochures, posters, local bus schedules, information about coming events, excursions, tours, and the availability of hotel rooms and apartments. Check with the friendly staff if you have any questions about the area.

Billiards - Billiard tables are in the new indoor tennis hall, open daily 9:00 am to midnight; tel: 74247 for reservations.

Bowling - Lanes are available in the new indoor tennis hall with four automatic alleys; tel: 74247. They are open every day from 9:00 am to midnight. There's outdoor bowling located near the outdoor tennis courts, open daily from 8:00 am to 8:00 pm.

Castles - The ruins of the 13th-century **Castle Wolkenstein** can be found at the entrance to the Vallunga/Langental, clinging to a high rock wall. It was acquired by Randolph von Villanders, who then called himself "von Wolkenstein" and who founded the mighty dynasty of the Counts of Wolkenstein. The castle was ruined in 1525 and never restored. The path up from the road to Vallunga/Langental is short, only a 15-minute walk, but it is very steep and not easy. The lovely **Castle Gardena/Fischburg** is located near Santa Cristina, below a wooded hillside, dominated by the peak of the Sassolungo. It was built between 1622 and 1641 when the old castle in Selva became uninhabitable. Bought and restored in 1926 by the current owner, Baron Franchetti of Venice, the castle cannot be entered, but views from the opposite hills of Santa Cristina are beautiful.

Churches - The **Parish Church of S. Maria ad Nivea** was originally built in 1878 in Neo-Gothic style and has been refurbished. The bell tower was built in 1678, and the original 1503 chapel was renovated in 1517, 1670 and 1789. The **Chapel of the Victims of the Mountain,** a small chapel with a carved wooden Pietà, is located in the local cemetery behind the church in Selva. Inside is a bronze book dedicated to those who have died on the mountains surrounding Selva.

Markets - General markets are held every Thursday morning in the hamlet of Plan, just outside of Selva, and every Friday morning in Ortesei and every Wednesday in S. Cristina.

Minigolf - Open daily 9:00 am to 10:00 pm.

Riding - Horseback riding is available in Plan from July through September.

Skating - An ice skating rink is located in the center of Selva behind the Gran Baita Hotel. Check with the Tourist Office for the schedule of hockey games.

Swimming, Sauna, Solarium - These are available for non-residents at the Hotels Antares, Gran Baita and Piccolo, all four-star hotels in Selva.

Tennis - New indoor courts are located in the ice arena building and are open daily from 9:00 am to 12 midnight; tel: 74247. Outdoor courts are open every day from 8:00 am to 8:00 pm.

Excursions in and around Selva/ Wolkenstein

This section introduces day excursions for *Easy Walkers* to enjoy when the weather is not suitable for high altitude walking, or if an alternative to walking is desired. Be sure to check current timetables for best connections if public transportation is used.

1. Lifts in and around Selva/Wolkenstein

A) Dantercepies - These gondolas rise to 7710 ft. (2350 m.) and provide superb views of the Sella group, Sassalungo, and into the Passo Sella/Grödner Joch. This lift is open from 8:30 am to 12:30 pm and 2:00 pm to 5:30 pm. (See Walk #2 for more details.)

Directions: The base lift station is on a hill above Selva. Check your village map and follow the signs to Dantercepies.

B) Ciampinoi - This gondola rises to 7481 ft. (2280 m.) and is open from 9:00 am to 12:15 pm and 2:00 pm to 6:00 pm. Like other lifts in the Selva area, views from the top are extraordinary. (See Walk #1 for more details.)

Directions: The lift station is on the main street of Selva, up from the Tourist Office.

C) Col Raiser - Slightly outside of Selva in Plan de Tieja, this gondola rises to 6890 ft. (2100 m.) on grassy alps with sensational views of Sassolunga. It is open from 8:30 am to 5:30 pm. (See Walk #4 for more details.)

Directions: Leave from the western end of Selva, walking on the highest auto road, towards S. Cristina, for the 40-minute walk to Plan da Tieja, where you follow the sign up to the right to the Col Raiser lift station.

2. Ortesei/St. Ulrich - With a population of about 5000, Ortesei is the largest village in the Val Gardena. Take advantage of its charming main street and piazza, with chic boutiques, restaurants and cafés, and then note:

A) Parish Church of Ortesei/St. Ulrich - This village church, built in Baroque style in the late 18th century, is dedicated to the "Three Kings" and St. Ulrich, bishop and patron saint of the village. Beautifully carved pews date from 1888, and the many ornately carved wood sculptures are the work of local wood-carvers and were made at the turn of this century.

B) Chapel of Remembrance - One of the oldest bells in the world hangs in the little facade tower of this chapel, situated near the parish church. The chapel commemorates the dead of the world wars, but the bell was found by a farmer and originally hung in the medieval castle of Stetteneck, no longer in existence.

C) Congress Hall and Permanent Exhibition of Gardenese Handicrafts - Visit the modern building on the church square where many evening events are held. On the ground floor is a permanent exhibit of local artisans—original works of wood-carvers as well as those of mass-production workshops—giving a clear picture of the wood-carver's art. On the ground floor of the Congress Hall is the Tourist Information office of Ortesei.

D) Church of St. Anthony - This lovely little church was built between 1673 and 1676 and is located across from the bus stop. Its steep shingle roof and onion dome make it a favorite of photographers.

E) Gardena Folk Museum - This musuem offers valuable insights into the culture of the Gardena Valley and includes handicrafts, folk culture, minerals and fossils, flora and fauna, paintings, and a documentation of the valley's 300-year-old art of wood-carving.

F) Train of the Val Gardena - The engine of the train which last ran on May 25, 1960, from Chiusa at 1769 ft. (539 m.) to Plan at 5312 ft. (1619 m.), is parked on the old railway tracks on the promenade behind the parish church. Finished in 1916, between WWI and WWII, the railroad was the main method of transporting goods and people in the valley, but by 1960 the line became unprofitable and was closed.

G) Lifts in Ortesei - The **Alpe di Siusi lift** links Ortesei with the slopes of the Siusi Alp (Alpe di Siusi/Seiser Alm), alpine pastures drenched with colorful fields of flowers, Europe's largest mountain pasture. Alpe di Siusi was developed as a major center for hikers in the 1970s. **Seceda** rises to 8039 ft. (2450 m.) and provides excellent, close-up views of nearby Dolomites and panoramas of the Val Gardena. **Chairlift Raschötz** rises to 6913 ft. (2107 m.) and is open 8:30 am to noon and 1:00 to 6:00 pm. **Bullaccia lift**, from the center of Ortesei, provides sweeping views of the Val Gardena towards the Sella group.

Directions: By car - Take the main road 242 northwest to Ortesei. Reverse directions to return. By "SAD" bus - buses leave Selva for Ortesei quite often in the morning (9:05, 9:25, 9:40, 9:55, 10:15 am) and return in the afternoon at 35 and 50 minutes past the hour until 5:00 pm, and continue to run frequently until 6:20 pm.

3. Bolzano/Bozen - 28 miles (45 km) from Selva, the capital of the autonomous province of Alto Adige is a quiet city at the meeting of the Isorco/Eisack and Talvera rivers.

The heart of Bolzano is the **Piazza Walther** walking street, named after a 12th-century, wandering German minstrel. At one corner of the square is the Gothic **Cathedral (Duomo)**, built between the 12th and 14th centuries. Take Via Posta from the other side of the square to Piazza Domenicani and visit the 13th-century **Dominican Church** with its paintings and frescoes. In adjoining **Cappelle di San Giovanni**, note the 14th-century frescoes.

Via Goethe leads to **Piazza della Erbe** and its imposing **statue of Neptune**. This piazza is home to a fruit and vegetable market every morning except Sunday, from 8:00 am to 1:00 pm, and is the beginning of Bolzano's main shopping street, **Via del Portici**, lined with narrow arcades. The **Museo Civico** houses a collection of traditional costumes, wood carvings and archaeological exhibits. Crossing the **Ponte Talvera** to Gries, visit the **Parish Church (Parrochiale)** with a 15th-century, carved wooden altar, then walk to the **Benedictine Abbey** and the **Church of Sant'Agostino**.

If time permits, you might enjoy an unusual excursion from Bolzano: a visit to the **Earth Pyramids**, a strange geological formation, a veritable forest of tall, thin, needle-like spires, each with a boulder on top, formed by erosion. These pyramids are on the Renon/Ritten Plateau, above Bolzano, and can be reached by way of the **Soprabolzano Funicular**, leaving from Via Renon, left of the Bolzano train station. At the end of this funicular, electric trains take visitors to Collalbo and the pyramids.

Directions: By car - Take main road 242 northwest through Ortesei, following the signs into Bolzano. Reverse directions to return. By bus - The 9:08 am bus arrives in Bolzano/Bozen at 10:30 am. To return to Selva, a 3:10 bus arrives at 4:57 pm, and the 4:40 bus arrives at 6:25 pm.

4. Bressanone/Brixen - The South Tyrol's largest city with a population of about 16,000, Bressanone is 22 miles

(35 km) northwest of Selva. The "old town" is small and easy to walk, with narrow alleys, lanes of arcades, patrician homes, stately churches and crumbling bridges, all dating from the Middle Ages.

The **Cathedral (Duomo)** was built in the 13th century and remodelled in the 18th century with Baroque interiors. The Gothic **Cloisters** were constructed about 1200, reconstructed in the 1300s and contain fine frescoes painted between 1390 and 1509. The Romanesque **Chapel of St. John the Baptist (San Giovanni Battista)**, dating from the 11th century, is at the southern end of the cloisters. The **Cathedral Treasury** can be reached from the cloisters and contains sacred robes and shrines. Walk to the late Renaissance **Palace of the Prince-Bishops (Palazzo Vescovile)** in the southwestern corner of the old town, over a bridge crossing a moat. You'll enjoy this small, charming city lying where the Rienz River flows into the Eisack River, and where the distinctive character of the South Tyrol first becomes apparent.

Directions: By car - Take the main road 242 northwest out of Selva, picking up 12 north and following signs into Bressanone/Brixen. Reverse directions to return. By bus - You can leave Selva at 9:43, arriving at Bressanone/Brixen at 10:50 am. To return to Selva, there is a 4:30 bus arriving at 5:42 pm.

5. Ponte Gardena - *Easy Walkers* can visit **Castle Trostburg** in Ponte Gardena, only 12 miles (19 km) from Selva. This ancient castle is at the valley entrance, high above Ponte Gardena/Waidbruck, and dates from the 12th century. It contains a superb Gothic room with a richly decorated, raftered ceiling. The library, one of the most famous of its time, and the banquet hall are also worth seeing. Access is by a path from Ponte Gardena, about a 30-minute uphill walk. Visiting hours and guided tours are given daily (except Monday) at 10:00 and 11:00 am, 2:00, 3:00 and 4:00 pm.

Directions: By bus - The 9:08 am bus arrives in Ponte Gardena at 10:00 am, and to return to Selva, there is a 2:54 bus arriving at 3:37 pm.

6. Puez-Odle Park - The 9400 hectares of this national park in the Dolomites include the village of Selva/Wolkenstein. The park is bounded by Mt. Putia to the northeast, Gardenaccia and Odle to the southwest, and Cir to the southeast. Note the spectacular contrast between the immense slopes of valleys and meadows and the sudden, almost vertical rise of the dolomite rocks. In the park, the Vallunga/Langental is the only example in the Dolomite region of an unspoiled, glacial valley. At the Vallunga's entrance are the ruins of Castle Wolkenstein on the Stevia rock wall, surrounded by high rocks that rise majestically from the valley's meadows. The alpine park flowers are varied, with crocus, snowdrop and anemone in spring; rhododendron, edelweiss, wood carnation and gentian in summer; along with the rare species of dwarf rhododendron, artemesia, rampion, red lily, wild saffron, wild Turkish lily and alpine poppy. The park is a peaceful, natural environment with spectacular scenery for all to enjoy. (See Walks #2 and #3 for more details.)

7. Venice - See the "Venice" chapter.

Directions: By car - Drive out of Selva on the main road 242 southeast to 42 east, picking up 51 south. North of Belluno on *autostrada* A27 south, follow signs to Venice. You'll go over a long causeway and arrive at a busy and confusing area, the Piazza Roma, a dead-end for car traffic. On your right is a pair of large, eight-story garages where you can park your car, but there can be a long line of cars trying to get into these garages if you don't arrive by 9:00 am. Walk from the garage across the top of Piazza Roma to the Grand Canal piers and take the large, inexpensive, public water bus or Vaporetto to San Marco. Reverse directions to return.

8. Merano/Meran - See the "Merano" chapter.

Directions: By car - 242 northwest through Orteseo to Bolzano where you will pick up 38 north into Merano. Reverse directions to return.

9. Cortina d'Ampezzo - See the chapter on "Cortina d'Ampezzo."

Directions: By car - Take the main road south and pick up 48 east over the Passo Pordoi and Passo Falzarego into Cortina. Reverse directions to return.

10. Innsbruck, Austria - The capital of the Tyrol province of Austria, 75 miles (120 km) north of Selva, combines the vitality of a modern town with the serenity of walking in the surrounding high mountains. If you arrive by train, turn left when you exit the station and check with the Tourist Office for city maps.

Among the important stops in Innsbruck are: **Hofburg Court Palace**, Rennweg 1, a sumptuous rococo palace; **Golden Roof (Goldenis Dachl)**, Herzog-Frederich-Strasse 14, there are 2657 gilded tiles on its Gothic oriels, built in the 15th century; **Olympic Museum** and the **City Tower (Stadtturn)**; **St. Jakob's Cathedral (Dom zu St. Jakob)**, Domplatz 6, a lavish, baroque cathedral rebuilt in the 1700s; **Court Church**, built in the mid-16th century with a wooden organ from 1600 that is still used today.

The **Tyrolean Folkloric Museum (Tiroler Volkskunst)**, Universitätsstrasse 2, the museum was first built as an abbey in 1553, was converted to a school in 1785 and then to a museum in 1929 and currently houses an important folkloric collection of costumes, furniture and art. Also worth a visit is the **Alpine Zoo (Alpenzee)**, Weiderburggasse 37, the highest-altitude zoo in Europe, featuring alpine animals in a natural environment. Take Tram 1 or 6 to the funicular railway, Hungerburgbahn and buy a round-trip ticket. Ride to and from the zoo as a free extra.

Directions: By car - 242 northwest through Ortesei, picking up *autostrada* A22 north over the Brenner Pass and the Austrian border. Follow the local signs into Innsbruck. Reverse directions to return. Remember your passport!

11. "SAD" Bus Tours - Prices and current timetables are available at the Tourist Office for trips to the following destinations: Venice, Cortina d' Ampezzo, Lago di Carezza/Karersee, Lake Garda, Merano/Lago de Caldaro, Innsbruck and Salzburg in Austria, and Munich and Neusch-wanstein Castle in Germany. Don't forget, if you leave Italy, take your passport!

Selva/Wolkenstein Walks

Recommended Map: Tabacco - Gröden-Seiseralm, Val Gardena-Alpe di Siusi

Walk #1: Selva Lift to Ciampinoi, Rifugio Comici to Rifugio Passo Sella to Plan de Gralba to Selva (Lift Excursion to Sassolungo)

Walking Easy Time
3½ hours
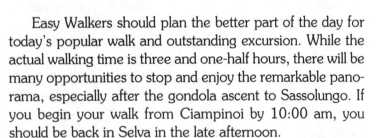

Easy Walkers should plan the better part of the day for today's popular walk and outstanding excursion. While the actual walking time is three and one-half hours, there will be many opportunities to stop and enjoy the remarkable pano-rama, especially after the gondola ascent to Sassolungo. If you begin your walk from Ciampinoi by 10:00 am, you should be back in Selva in the late afternoon.

The day begins at Selva, taking the gondola to Ciampinoi at 7395 ft. (2254 m.), and the walk proceeds in the direction of the Rifugio Comici at 7064 ft. (2153 m.). Here you will be rewarded with close-up views of the east wall of the Sassolungo, rising to 10,437 ft. (3181 m.). Your destination is Rifugio Passo Sella at 7153 ft. (2180 m.), where you have the option of taking the gondola lift up on the Sassolungo at 8796 ft. (2681 m.) for extended views of the Dolomites.

The return to Selva is on a descending trail, through the hamlet of Plan de Gralba at 5870 ft. (1789 m.) and continuing all the way to Selva at 5118 ft. (1560 m.). This hike is considered "comfortable," as most of the walking is not difficult, with ascents and descents at a reasonable rate. There are sections that are rocky and will take some maneuvering, but *Easy Walkers* can accomplish this outing with no problem. There are many options for good food at the *rifugios*, but a picnic on the meadow is the best option of all.

Directions: The Ciampinoi lift station can be easily found on the main street of Selva. Purchase a one-way ticket to the top station for the ten-minute gondola ride.

Start: The hike begins at Ciampinoi. Walk towards the impressive Sassalungo massif in front of you and follow the signs to Rif. Comici and the Passo Sella Joch. After about ten minutes of walking around the mountain, the trail will descend to the valley below on a steep path, eased by terraced steps, bringing you to the foot of Sassalungo.

The path forks, the left trail being the short way to Plan de Gralba, but *Easy Walkers* will continue ahead towards the right to Rifugio Comici. The well-beaten trail splits again—continue to the left in the direction of the *rifugio*. After a comfortable 40-minute walk you will reach the sun terrace of Rifugio Comici for a rest before continuing on to the Sella Pass.

When ready, walk directly through the sun terrace, exiting onto a rocky trail blazed in red and white, signed "Passo Sellajoch 526." This path traverses open meadows with herds of friendly cows and jagged peaks edging the sky. If you look carefully you might see rock climbers in action along the trail. In the last fifteen minutes before reaching Passo Sella the trail becomes more rocky as it ascends, but it should present no problems for *Easy Walkers*—just take it at a slower pace. You should reach the *rifugio* at the top of the Sella Pass after about two hours of walking. At the side of the *rifugio* is a small chapel with benches, a nice place for a picnic if it is lunchtime.

Ahead on the right of the *rifugio* is a small, stand-up gondola lift that rises to a *rifugio* on the Sassolungo at 8796 ft. (2681 m.). We do not recommend any walking on top, just sensational viewing of the entire Sella group and extended views of the Grödner Joch.

After returning to the base station, the walk to Selva returns on trail #657 to Plan de Gralba, descending through the valley, not very far from the twisting auto road up on the right. From the Rifugio Passo Sella, walk down the auto road against the traffic flow, and about five minutes below the *rifugio* a sign directs you left on trail #657. Turn left on a

Selva 1560m.
End of Walk

Start of Walk
Ciampinoi
2254m.

Ciampinoi Lift

Plan de
Gralba
1789m.

Rif. Comici
2153m.

#657

Sassolungo
3181m.

#526

Rif.
Sassolungo
2681m.

Rif. Passo
Sella
2180m.

Lift

small, unpaved road, and when the split rail fence ends on the right, turn right on to an **unmarked** path. After a few hundred yards the path will be blazed #657. Follow it all the way down to Plan de Gralba at 5870 ft. (1789 m.), with some nice restaurants and sun terraces.

Walk through Plan de Gralba on a small country road past two closed lifts on your left. Just after the second lift, make a left turn over a little bridge, and after a few hundred feet, turn right on an **unmarked**, wide, descending gravel path (actually a ski trail), leading to the small hamlet of Fungeia. Continue walking straight ahead, staying on the left of the stream on a small, paved auto road as you walk into Selva.

Walk #2: Selva/Dantercepies Lift, Walk Dantercepies to Rifugio Clark through Pra de Frea to Rifugio Forcelles to Passo Gardena to Plan to Selva

Walking Easy Time
3½ to 5 hours

The walk from Dantercepies at 7540 ft. (2298 m.) to Rifugio Forcelles at 6893 ft. (2101 m.), through the Passo Gardena/Grödner Joch, is filled with views of craggy, dolomitic peaks on both sides of the Pass, and the path passes along the edge of the Naturpark Puez-Geisler. As if that weren't enough, the hypnotic face of Sassolungo dominates the panorama on the return hike.

Walkers and climbers seem to be everywhere on well-marked paths rolling easily through meadows, scrambling up and down rocky mountain trails. Plan a full day for this walk, as you will want to spend at least one hour having a picnic lunch on a sunny meadow, perhaps watching climbers ascending the craggy peaks of the mountains above, and another hour for resting, photography and scenery-viewing.

From trails winding along the mountain, walkers can see the twisting auto road snaking through the pass from Selva to Colfusco. In fact, many hikers continue on from Rifugio Forcelles past the Restaurant Edelweiss, taking the lift down to Colfusco, where you can catch a bus back to Selva through the pass. Today's itinerary though, is to have *Easy Walkers* return on the same trail from Forcelles, meeting the path to the Rifugio Passo Gardena, and then descending through the beautiful valley and forest to the hamlet of Plan at 5266 ft. (1605 m.) and along a pleasant *spazierweg* to Selva.

While this hike is considered "comfortable," there are a few extended rocky descents that are not dangerous, but require some care. Frequent rest stops should be taken as downhill walking can bring stress to the knees.

Directions: Check your Selva village map and walk up to the Dantercepies Lift Station at 5397 ft. (1645 m.). Buy a one-way ticket to Dantercepies and take the continuously moving gondola for the ten-minute ride to the top. At the top lift station at 7540 ft. (2298 m.), walkers can view the Passo Gardena/Grödner Joch down on the right and climbers scrambling up jagged peaks up to the left.

Start: *Easy Walkers* will follow the sign to the Rif. Clark down steps to the left, reaching the sun terrace of this tiny restaurant in only 15 minutes. Path #2 goes up to the left in the direction of Rif. Puez at 8121 ft. (2475 m.), but this climb is not on today's agenda. Instead, walk to the right, following the signs to Forcelles and then Colfusco, over a little grassy path and by a ski lift, on to a narrow, rocky, descending trail. This trail is somewhat steep and descends

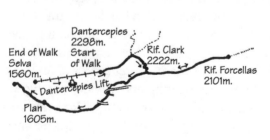

from 7290 ft. (2222 m.) to 6890 ft. (2100 m.) through a scrubby pine forest in about one-half hour. It is not dangerous but takes some care going down. The trail eventually meets the Passo Gardena path, but now you will turn left in the direction of Rif. Forcelles on a pretty trail that can bring hikers all the way to Colfusco. After walking through the meadows for about 15 minutes, a perfect picnic opportunity arises—a bench with a delightful panoramic view.

> ☞ **HINT: If you wish, after your picnic, you can shorten today's hike by not going on to the Rif. Forcelles, but by returning on the same path and walking ahead at the intersection, where you came down earlier, in the signed direction of Passo Gardena.**

For those that wish to continue, the Forcelles trail ascends a bit to 6890 ft. (2100 m.), where after a rest, you will return along the same trail, following the sign to Passo Gardena. The Passo Gardena is the high point for auto traffic through the pass at 6969 ft. (2124 m.).

The trail comes to a barn and tiny farmhouse. You can turn left and continue down to the road and then up to the Passo Gardena, however, a turn to the right past the little house brings you to a narrow mountain path on your left. Follow this trail, ending up at a souvenir stand on the main road. Turn right and walk on the road to the second group of buildings and the Rifugio Passo Gardena on the left (which serves some great Austrian specialties—*kaiserschmarrn*, *knoedlsuppe* and *bratwurst*.)

Continue walking on the road, on the right side, and after a few minutes you'll see the sign "Selva #654." Turn right on this path, descending gently through a serene, grassy meadow, passing old barns with farmers haying, leading into a more steeply descending forest path. Watch for signs to Selva and blazes of #654. The trail ends at an auto road.

Follow the sign to Selva around to the right of the road, down to the hamlet of Plan, again meeting the auto road. Turn right and walk down the road for a few minutes. Enter a parking area on the right, next to a sports field, and look for the sign to the left reading "Passeggiata" and "Spazier-weg." This is a little paved path up above the auto road down on the left. Stay on this paved path until the very end in

Selva. It brings you into the parking area of the Sun Valley Hotel where you turn left down the road, making a right turn at the corner to the church and to your hotel.

Walk #3: Selva, in the Parco Naturale Puez-Odle, through the Vallunga/Langental, Return to Selva

Walking Easy Time
3 to 5 hours

The hike through the Vallunga valley can be reserved for a cloudy or drizzly day, as no lifts are involved. You will walk into the Vallunga Valley (Langental), the only unspoiled glacial valley in the Parco Naturale Puez. The trail ascends gently from 5355 ft. (1632 m.) to 6890 ft. (2100 m.), and then climbs seriously into the rugged Dolomites at the Rifugio Puez at 8121 ft. (2475 m.).

But today, *Easy Walkers* will walk only as far as they feel comfortable, remembering that a two-hour walk ascending into the valley will be about a one and one-half hour return. The early part of the trail winds through open, grassy meadows filled with many picnic opportunities and eventually works its way

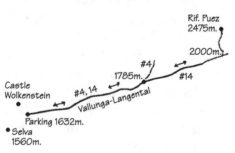

through a narrow pass with towering mountains on each side, climbing to high peaks at the distant end. The return to Selva is along the same path.

There are no restaurants or facilities in the valley, except for those experienced walkers who hike up to the Rifugio Puez, so remember to pack a picnic lunch.

Directions: *Easy Walkers* can either drive or walk to the start of today's hike. There is a small parking area at the beginning of the trail. Please follow the Selva village map to the large "P" (parking) just below and past Castle Wolkenstein at the entrance to the valley and the nature park.

Start: If you are walking, you will follow the signs to Vallunga/Langental. Check the village map.

Enter the park at the end of the parking area on trail #4-14. This is the main and only path that goes deeply into the valley, starting at 5355 ft. (1632 m.). As you walk through the meadow, note the tiny, early 18th-century chapel, recently restored. Take a few minutes to enter and discover the old frescoes and lovely altar inside. The trail proceeds, ascending through the valley on a popular, rocky path. Trail #4 splits off to the left, ascending steeply into the Puez Alps, but you will continue ahead on #14, as long as you feel comfortable. At 6890 ft. (2100 m.), the trail ascends dramatically up to the Rifugio Puez. Most *Easy Walkers* will then reverse direction and return to Selva on the same path.

Walk #4: Selva to Plan da Tieja, Col Raiser Lift, Col Raiser to Gamsblut to St. Jakob/San Giacomo Church to Ortesei/St. Ulrich

 Walking Easy Time
3½ hours

Today's hike brings *Easy Walkers* from Selva at 5118 ft. (1560 m.), through the Val Gardena by way of Col Raiser, to the village of Ortesei/St. Ulrich at 4692 ft. (1430 m.). Plan the better part of a day for today's hike, as you will first take a 40-minute walk up to the Col Raiser lift in the village of Plan da Tieja, then take the gondola up to Col Raiser and

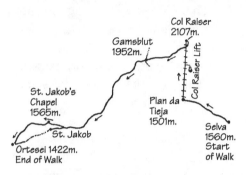

walk around the mountain to Ortesei, stopping at the ancient church above St. Jakob, finally returning Selva by bus.

The top lift station at Col Raiser 6890 ft. (1430 m.), sits in the midst of a grassy plain, surrounded by the Dolomites, with exciting views of Sassolungo. The walk continues to Ortesei by way of an unused road, through meadows and forest, with a stop above St. Jakob to visit the church. In this area paths are well-marked and well-engineered. There is a restaurant with large sun terrace and facilities at the top station of Col Raiser and another restaurant at Gamsblut, however, a picnic lunch in the meadow would also be enjoyable today.

Start: Leave from the western end of Selva, walking on the highest auto road, signed towards S. Cristina, for the 40-minute walk to Plan da Tieja, where you follow the sign up to the right to the Col Raiser lift station. Purchase a one-way ticket to Col Raiser and take the continuously moving gondola for the ten-minute ride to Col Raiser.

The Col Raiser restaurant, with its extra-large sun terrace and cafeteria, sits in the middle of a tranquil, grassy alp. Views from this point are sensational, with new views of Sassolungo, and jagged peaks to the north and east. There are several hikes from Col Raiser to *rifugios* in the area, but today *Easy Walkers* will leave Col Raiser by following the sign (at the far side of the sun-terrace as you enter it) marked "Gamsblut" and "St. Jakob" on #4.

The narrow, well-maintained path leaves from the side of the terrace, descending somewhat steeply at first, to the restaurant Gamsblut at 6405 ft. (1952 m.), on path #4. After passing the restaurant, walk on path #4 into the forest, following the unused jeep road down and around the mountain, following signs to the church at St. Jakob.

You will have to leave the trail and walk to the right at a signed intersection to visit the chapel at 5135 ft. (1565 m.), sitting above the little hamlet of St. Jakob. This church is the oldest in the valley and dates back to the mid-13th century. Its original Romanesque interior was added to, and the present church dates back to the Gothic period, with both Gothic and Baroque interior decoration. Many of the sculptures are excellent local copies, with originals in the Gardena Folk Museum in Ortesei. Descend through the larch trees overlooking the village of St. Jakob and rejoin the trail into the village of Ortesei. (See Excursion #2 for details on what to do and see in Ortesei.)

Walk #5: Ortesei Alpe di Siusi/Seiser Alm Lift, Walk Top Station to Saltaria to Santa Cristina

Walking Easy Time
3½ hours

Easy Walkers should leave five to six hours for today's hike which crosses Europe's largest alp (meadowland), framed by the western wall of Sassolungo and other dramatic Dolomite peaks of the Südtirol. Today's hike should be taken on a clear day, when every mountain appears to be finely etched against a brilliant blue sky.

You will take the bus from Selva at 5118 ft. (1560 m.) to Ortesei at 4055 ft. (1236 m.), traveling through Santa Cristina (passing the bus stop you will use to return to Selva at the conclusion of today's hike). Ortesei is the major village in the Val Gardena, flowing over with shops and hotels, churches and museums, hosting two lifts that take summer walkers up to the mountains on both sides of the valley. Today, you will take the Alpe di Siusi Funivie (cable car) to 6578 ft. (2005 m.) and walk through one of the most picturesque alps in Europe. Rolling green meadows stretch to the horizon, framed by the jagged peaks of the Dolomites.

It will take about one hour and fifteen minutes to descend gently through the Alpe di Siusi/Seiser Alm to the auto road at Saltaria at 5597 ft. (1706 m.). Walkers then have the option of taking the covered chairlift up to Williamshütte at

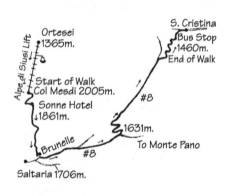

6890 ft. (2100 m.) for remarkable panoramic views of the Alpe di Siusi, or continuing through the natural wilderness and deep gorge of the Jëndertal to S. Cristina at 4685 ft. (1428 m.), and the short bus ride to Selva.

Directions: Take one of the frequent "SAD" buses from Selva (in front of the post office or down from the Hotel des Alpes on the main street) to Ortesei. After leaving the bus, walk across the river on a small bridge, turning right in the direction of the lift.

After a five-minute walk to the cable car station, purchase a one-way ticket to the Alpe di Siusi. The top station has a large restaurant, sun terrace and facilities. The directional signs are straight ahead as you exit the cable car.

Start: Follow the sign to the left to Saltaria on a well-graded path. The path descends to the four-star hotel Sonne (with restaurant and facilities) and proceeds through the tranquil Alpe di Siusi/Seiser Alm to Saltaria at 5597 ft. (1706 m.). While this part of the hike takes about one and one-quarter hours, you might wish to spend some time on the trail absorbing the beauty of this tranquil setting with its panoramas of the Sassolungo and Sciliar. At Saltaria (where there is a restaurant and facilities), you have the option of walking around on the road, up to the lift to Williamshütte, ascending to 6890 ft. (2100 m.) for lunch or picnic and views of the plateau below.

When ready, return to the lift base station, turning left and then right, following the sign to Jëndertal on a small mountain road passing in front of the Brunelle Hotel. This path is blazed #8/3a as you pass a picturesque old farmhouse selling milk and honey. At the first intersection, cross the river on the little bridge to the right. This comfortable path continues through the forest with the river on your left and rises up to another intersection at 5351 ft. (1631 m.). If you haven't eaten lunch, a conveniently placed bench at the top of this ascent is a welcome sight.

Follow the sign down to the left to S. Cristina and Ortesei. You are now walking on a well-defined path down through the natural, unspoiled wilderness of the Jëndertal, above the river as it runs rapidly through its narrow gorge to S. Cristina. Exit this path onto a small, paved auto road with views of S. Cristina down to the right. From the road, turn right and take the signed "S. Cristina" hillside path descending steeply through the meadows to the paved auto road. Turn right and quickly left, walking up and around on the small road, directly to the main auto road in front of you. At the road, proceed left for a few meters to the bus stop, with frequent service posted to Selva.

Walk #6: Ortesei Chairlift Raschötz to Ega di Cason, Walk to Rifugio Brogles to Mid-Station Seceda Lift

Walking Easy Time
3½ hours

Today's walk starts and ends in Ortesei, involving the chairlift Raschötz, with a top station at 6890 ft. (2100 m.), and a walk on a continuously ascending and descending path on Seceda's upper plains. You will travel all the way to the Rifugio Brogles, on the back side of Seceda, with fabulous views of the Odle/Geisler Range and its highest peak, Sas Rigais, at 9925 ft. (3025 m.). The walk continues to a high point of 7008 ft. (2136 m.) and then descends through

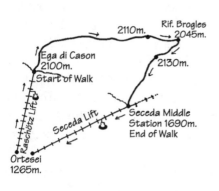

meadow and forest to the mid-station of the Seceda cable car for the quick descent to Ortesei and the bus return to Selva. If you haven't visited Ortesei, this is a good opportunity to do so. (See Excursion #2 for more details on Ortesei.)

Directions: Take one of the frequent morning buses to Ortesei. Walk up to the north, following the signs to the Sesselift Raschötz, and purchase a ticket to the top.

Start: There are several walks from the top station of this chairlift, all clearly signed. One walk goes west on path #35 to the Raschötzhütte at 7120 ft. (2170 m.); another starts on path #35 but quickly switches on path #7 at 6926 ft. (2111 m.) to the mid-station of the Seceda cable car. Today *Easy Walkers* will follow the signs on #35 in a northerly direction to Rifugio Brogles at 6710 ft. (2045 m.). This trail is well defined and offers sensational views of the Odle range.

After some rest and perhaps lunch at the *rifugio*, follow path #3, climbing a bit at first, but then descending all the way to 5545 ft. (1690 m.) at the middle station of the Seceda cable car. Purchase a one-way ticket down to Ortesei and catch the return bus to Selva.

Walk #7: Ortesei to Top Station Seceda, Col Raiser via the "Restaurant Route," Optional Walk to Selva

Walking Easy Time
2 to 4 hours
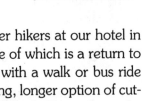

This walk was suggested by other hikers at our hotel in Selva and offers several options, one of which is a return to Plan da Tieja above Santa Cristina with a walk or bus ride back to Selva, or the more challenging, longer option of cutting below the Col Raiser lift at the Rifugio Fermeda to the restaurant at Juac and a downhill trek into Selva.

Directions: Take the morning bus from Selva to Ortesei and the Seceda cable car lift, following signs from the bus stop in Ortesei. Purchase a one-way ticket to the top station at Seceda, 8058 ft. (2456 m.), where the walk begins.

Start: *Easy Walkers* will pass a variety of *ristorantes* and *rifugios* on this hike, with the possibility of putting a few pounds on rather than taking them off, considering the local specialties served at these mountain restaurants. After taking in the view at Seceda, walk to the right, facing the Seceda mountain range, to Ristorante Sophie at 7914 ft. (2412 m.). Continue down to the right on #6 and make a left turn at the intersection to Ristorante Mastlé at 7494 ft. (2284 m.).

Start of Walk
Seceda 2456m.
Sophie 2412m.
Rist. Daniel 2228m.
Mastlé
Rif. Fermeda 2111m.
Seceda Lift
Mid-Station 1690m.
Col Raiser 2107m.
End of Short Walk
Option A
Juac 1903m.
Option B
Ortesei 1365m.
Plan da Tieja
Selva 1560m.
End of Full Walk

Proceed to Ristorante Daniel at 7310 ft. (2228 m.), under one of the Seceda ski lifts, then descend further to Rifugio Fermeda at 6926 ft. (2111 m.). At the intersection just past Rifugio Fermeda, walk on path #2 in the direction of the lift station at Col Raiser at 6913 ft. (2107 m.), for the descent by gondola to Plan da Tieja at 4925 ft. (1501 m.). Walk down the hill on the road and turn right, following the signs to S. Cristina to catch one of the frequent buses to Selva.

For those who don't mind some additional downhill walking, there is an option while on trail #2, that can be exercised just before you turn down to the Col Raiser gondola. You can continue ahead on trail #2 to Rifugio Firenze/Regensbergerhütte at 6683 ft. (2037 m.), following jeep trail #3 down to Juac at 6244 ft. (1903 m.), and staying on #3 and descending all the way into Selva.

There are dozens of variations of walks around Selva in the Val Gardena. *Easy Walkers* are encouraged to check the local hiking map and plot their own itineraries, making sure they note the ascents and descents carefully.

CORTINA D'AMPEZZO

Spectacular! There is no lens but that of the human eye that can catch and truly comprehend the stark grandeur of the Dolomites of Cortina d'Ampezzo, and even that fine instrument can sometimes be overwhelmed by the majesty of Cortina's compelling surroundings. In summer, dramatic sunsets silhouette the gigantic ruptures of earth and stone, the soft verdure of the Ampezzo Valley lying snugly within these finely etched mountains. Photographers must surely experience intense emotions as they try to capture this ever-shifting, almost primeval scene on film. The colors of the landscape change constantly as the sun moves across the sky, the azure lakes reflect the hard-edged peaks. The delicate green meadows ablaze with wildflowers versus the unforgiving, jagged rock formations make for an intriguing dichotomy. *Easy Walkers* are in for the time of their lives—seven days of walking in the incomparable beauty of the Dolomites and casual evenings strolling the pedestrian street in the elegant town of Cortina d'Ampezzo.

The first outsiders to visit the Ampezzo Valley were mountain climbers hearing about Cortina from Deodat de Dolomieu, the French geologist who first described these soaring peaks. Foreign tourists soon followed, spreading stories about the wondrous sights around Cortina, and the town became famous, in winter for its incomparable skiing, in summer for its mountain climbing and hiking. Cortina attracted illustrious guests—kings, princes, movie stars, politicians, authors and business leaders. It was, and still is, chic to see and be seen in Cortina, and almost all visitors stroll up and down the Corso (pedestrian thoroughfare) between 5:00 and 7:00 pm, filling the stores, window shopping or sipping a pre-dinner aperitif at la Post Hotel, on this fashionable street lined with hotels, art galleries, antique shops, jewelers, boutiques, cafés and restaurants. Grand hotels built in the 1920s and 30s lend an elegant touch to Cortina, and the hills above are dotted with the charming country chalets of important Italian families who come to Cortina for winter sports and August holiday.

Cortina is a different kind of base village for *Easy Walkers*—the streets crowded with "the beautiful people," rather than hikers and backpackers—but Cortina's Dolomite trails are still filled with walkers, hikers, backpackers and mountain climbers. Cortina may be more expensive than other Italian base villages during the month of August, so *Easy Walkers* should consider the month of July and the first ten days of September for their Cortina d'Ampezzo walking holiday.

Cortina, at 3970 ft. (1210 m.), is surrounded by many peaks over 10,500 ft. (3200 m.). Many visitors arriving in Cortina for the first time are stunned by the magnificent sight of these surrounding Dolomites—the mountain groups of Tofana, Pomagagnon, Cristallo, Sorapis and Croda da Lago—and the Boite river running through the town. The eastern slopes of the Pomagagnòna and Punta Fiames mountains are spectacular at sunset; Cristallo sparkles in the afternoon sun; and Tofana gleams golden in the early morning sunrise. Cortina was the scene of the 1956 winter Olympic Games and has 45 lifts spread over varied slopes surrounding this beautiful valley. While these lifts service a network of over 62 miles (100 km) of ski runs and cross-country trails, many lifts also operate in summer, bringing hikers to the beginning of fascinating day walks.

It is difficult to believe that Cortina is only a two-hour drive from the wonders of Venice, and *Easy Walkers* can also experience a one- or two-day walking itinerary in this magical city. Twisting, scenic mountain roads also take travelers from Cortina through the Dolomites, off the beaten track south to Alleghe's beautiful lake, and for a visit to the Agordino. A drive west through the Passo Pordoi brings walkers to the Val di Fassa and Vigo di Fassa, in another *Walking Easy* valley. Cortina is only 40 minutes from the Austrian border, close enough to Lienz, Austria, for an interesting one-day excursion.

In August, Cortina is filled with happy Italian families who come for the healthy, dry climate and the hiking. The trails here are varied enough to meet the needs of all levels of walkers—supported by a multiple-lift system providing easy and exciting ways to visit the many *rifugios* in the surrounding mountains. Explore the dozens of places around Cortina which offer *Easy Walkers* a variety of paths and scenery—from the solitude of a walk through the forest to Rifugio Mietres to the pleasant company of dozens of hikers around Tre Cimi, from the silent chairlift rising above peaceful Lake Misurina to the large, three-stage cable car called "The Arrow in the Sky," rising to 10,640 ft. (3243 m.) at Tofane de Mezzo.

The Azienda Promozione Turistica of Cortina (Cortina Tourist Office) and organizations such as Consorzio per lo Sviluppo Turistico di Cortina (Cortina Holidays), provide a first-rate, cultural, social and sporting environment for summer visitors. A *Walking Easy* trip to the Italian Alps should definitely include the "Queen of the Dolomites," Cortina d'Ampezzo.

Transportation to Cortina d'Ampezzo

By Plane: There are international airports at Munich, Germany, 217 miles (350 km) from Cortina, and Milan, Italy. However, a change of plane can bring you into Venice, only 105 miles (170 km) south of Cortina and an easy two-hour car ride. Car rental agencies are located at each airport.

By Rail: Cortina's closest train station is at Dobbiaco/Toblach, 19 miles (30 km) to the north. Local bus service to Cortina and car rentals are available.

By Bus: There is direct service to Cortina from Munich, Milan, Venice and other major cities. There is also local bus service in the Cortina area on the Autobus Cortina d'Ampezzo.

Sample Bus Timetables:

Dep. Milan	7:10 am
Arr. Cortina	2:55 pm
Dep. Dobbiaco/Toblach	2:00 pm
Arr. Cortina	2:45 pm

By Car: From the west and north, exit *autostrada* A22 at Brixen-Pustertal and take 49 towards Dobbiaco/Toblach, driving south on 51 to Cortina.

From the east and southeast, take 51 from near Pieve di Cadore to Cortina. Or, 52 from Santo Stefano di Cadore, turning west on 48 to Auronzo and then to Cortina.

From local areas in the Dolomites, use local roads over the Passo Pordoi and Passo Sella, or Passo Pordoi to Passo Falzarego, continuing on to Cortina d'Ampezzo.

The Grand Strada delle Dolomiti, the Great Dolomite Road from Ora/Auer east to Cortina d'Ampezzo (State Highway #48), was opened in 1909, a remarkable engineering feat linking some of the most dramatic parts of the Dolomites. The road passes through varied landscapes of unrivalled beauty and traverses high, stark passes and green, peaceful valleys. Leaving Ora, the first pass crossed is Passo San Lugano at 3612 ft. (1101 m.), then the Val di Fiemme and the Val di Fassa (Cavalese, Predazzo, Moena, Canazei), climbing to the highest point on the road at Passo Pordoi

7346 ft. (2239 m.). The road descends in wide curves with fabulous views of the surrounding mountains—on the left passing by the Sella group and on the right by Padòn, behind which Marmolada and its glacier can be seen.

At the foot of the pass is the summer and winter resort of Arabba at 5256 ft. (1602 m.), with a network of cable cars and chairlifts, a fabulous view of the Marmolada glacier and a 17th-century church, now a national monument. Further along the road, past Arabba, high on the mountainside at 4807 ft. (1465 m.), stands the little village of Livinallongo, with breathtaking views of the Civetta, Pelmo, Marmolada and the Sella.

At 4685 ft. (1428 m.) is the hamlet of Andraz, a cluster of old alpine houses and the ruins of a 10th-century castle perched on a rocky spur which can be seen on the winding road to Falzarego. This pass is at 6907 ft. (2105 m.) and has a cable car rising to 9010 ft. (2746 m.) at Lagazuoi on the left, and the much-photographed climbing rocks of Cinque Torri on the right. (See Walk #6.) As the pass descends towards Cortina you proceed through Pocol at 5010 ft. (1527 m.), and when the car comes out of the Crepa Tunnel, suddenly in front of you is a splendid view of the Valle d'Ampezzo and Cortina d'Ampezzo, your destination.

Activities in Cortina d'Ampezzo

This section lists activities available in Cortina when additions or alternatives to walking are desired. Cortina's Tourist Office (Azienda Promozione Turistica) is located on Piazetta San Francesco, 8; tel: 436/3231.

Biking - Bicycles may be rented along the road at Fiames, the starting point of many excursions, and in town.

Churches - Visit the lovely baroque parish church built in 1775 with its 243-foot-high (74 m.) bell tower rising over the rooftops as the village landmark. It is located on Cortina's pedestrian street, in the heart of town.

"Cortina No Limits" - This company is an association of professionals who founded a school to provide people with a chance to enjoy certain sports activities that previously were reserved for skilled athletes. "Cortina No Limits" instructors, all licensed professionals, offer canyoning, rafting, kayaking, snow rafting and "Taxi Bob," a uniquely thrilling bobsled experience. For more information, call 436-860808.

Cultural and Sporting Activities - There are band and choir concerts and folk groups, with participants wearing local costumes. The yearly presentation of the Cortina Ulisse literary prize, the Coppa d'Oro delle Dolomiti period-car race (held the first weekend in September) and the Italian Cricket championship are other big events locally. Check with the Tourist Office.

Fishing - Trout are plentiful in the Boite River running through Cortina, and in surrounding mountain lakes. Check with the Tourist Office for fishing permits.

Fitness Course - The course begins at Cademai and follows the route of the former railroad tracks.

Golf - The nine-hole golf course is located at the Hotel Miramonte Majestic, with a driving range at Guargnè, near the bottom station of the chairlift to Mietres.

Minigolf - You can play miniature golf at the course on Via del Castello.

Museums - The **Museum of Modern Art (Mario Rimoldi)** houses a remarkable collection of modern art, including paintings and sculptures from some of the major Italian representatives of art in the 1900s. The **Paleontologic Museum (Rinaldo Zardini)** contains millions of years of earth's history, a remarkable collection of marine fossils from the region of the Dolomites surrounding Cortina. The **Ethnological Museum of Ampezzo** is actually a museum of tradition—exhibiting crafts, costumes and daily work habits of people living long ago in the Ampezzo Valley. The museums are all situated in the same building at Ra Ciasa de ra Regoles, or Regole di Cortina D'Ampezzo, located off the pedestrian street near the church and supported by a group interested in preserving the ethnic inheritance of the Ampezzo Valley.

Riding - Use the stables of Fattoria Meneguto, near the Baita Fraina. They have a riding school and also organize excursions.

Skating - The Olympic Ice Skating rink is next to the Tofane Lift Station and skating, skate rental and lessons are available.

Swimming - A large indoor swimming pool with solarium is at Guargnè, next to the chairlift to Col Tondo and Miétres.

Tennis - There is one indoor court and several outdoor courts at the Tennis Country Club, Sopiazes.

Excursions in and around Cortina d'Ampezzo

This section introduces day-excursions for *Easy Walkers* to enjoy when the weather is not suitable for high-altitude walking, or if an alternative to walking is desired. Be sure to check current timetables if using public transportation.

1. Lifts in and around Cortina d'Ampezzo

A) Tondi di Faloria - A two-stage cable car leaving every half-hour, this lift brings *Easy Walkers* to 7667 ft. (2343 m.) and dramatic views of Cortina, and the Tofane, Sorapis and Cristallo mountains. The base station is near the bus terminal. (See Walk #4 for more details.)

B) Tofana di Mezzo - This awesome, three-stage cable car rises to 10,673 ft. (3244 m.) every half-hour. Called "Arrow in the Sky," it was built in 1969, with its base station near Stadio del Ghiacco (the Olympic ice rink). The first stage rises to 5578 ft. (1700 m.) at Col Drusciè with an observatory and restaurant. The second stage continues to 8990 ft. (2740 m.) at Ra Valles, with many scenic vistas and exciting hiking trails. The view from the third stage at the top offers panoramas extending into the Austrian mountains, the Central Alps and the Po Plains. (See Walk #3 for more details.)

C) Lagazuoi - The Lagazuoi chairlift and cable car can be accessed from Passo Falzarego, west of Cortina. The view from the top is considered the best panorama of the Dolomites, and in the distance are the Civetta, Pelmo, Marmolada, Gruppo Sella and the Pale di San Martino mountains, in addition to the peaks surrounding Cortina.

D) Cinque Torri - Located on route 48 to Passo Falzarego, before reaching the Lagazuoi cable car, this chairlift to 7763 ft. (2366 m.), affords spectacular, close-up views of the surrounding mountains. "Cinque Torri" are five towers of vertical rock, not particularly tall, but used by climbers to train for the high peaks because they range in difficulty from easy to very difficult. The most popular rock tower is a fourth-level climb named "Miriam"! (See Walk #6 for more details.)

E) Cristallo - This single chairlift, located on the road to Misurina, can take *Easy Walkers* up to San Forca at 7333 ft. (2235 m.), with transfer to a gondola rising to the jagged peaks of Cristallo at 9502 ft. (2896 m.) and stunning panoramic views. (See Walk #4 for more details.)

F) Mietres, Col Tondo - The double chairlift rises first to Col Tondo, then to the *rifugio* and Mietres, with its outstanding views of the Pomagagnon range. (See Walk #4 for more details.)

2. Pocol - Pocol is a tiny suburb outside of Cortina, on the Falzerago Pass road. Follow signs and walk to the **Belvedere** at 5049 ft. (1539 m.), where the panoramic view of the Ampezzo Valley and its surrounding peaks is best seen at sunset. Nearby is the **Sacrario**, containing the remains of 10,000 soldiers who died in World War I.

Directions: Bus service is available from Cortina every hour. By car - Follow signs to Passo Falzarego.

3. Pieve di Cadore - At 2881 ft. (878 m.), this pretty town of 4200, located southeast of Cortina, is one of the oldest holiday resorts in the Dolomites and has drawn walkers and mountain lovers from the mid-19th century. Pieve de Cadore is the birthplace of the famous Renaissance painter Titian, born in 1478—his home may be visited in Pieve along with the **Parish Church** containing one of his paintings. Note also the old **Magnifica Comunità del Cadore** building in the center of the village, with its beautiful rooms, and the **Cadore Museum**'s Roman and Venetian archaeological exhibits.

Directions: By car - 51 south from Cortina (in the direction of Venice) into Pieve. Reverse directions to return.

4. Dobbiaco/Toblach - Lying north of Cortina in the Val Pusteria or Pustertal, this busy Tyrolean village of 2700 is a good base for exploring the Sesto/Sexten region of northern Italy. Dobbiaco lies at the junction of several valleys and on the road to the northern Dolomite areas. Note the town's characteristic old houses and stop in at the Rococco **Parish Church**, dating from 1782, with its stucco work and magnificent ceiling frescoes. The Austrian composer Gustav Mahler frequently stayed in this area, where he composed his ninth and tenth symphonies. *Easy Walkers* might enjoy taking the **Mt. Radsberg Chairlift** to the 5269 ft. (1606 m.) summit for vistas of the Sesto/Sexten Dolomites and the Höhlenstein Valley.

Directions: By car - 51 north into Dobbiaco. Reverse directions to return. By bus - The 8:50 bus arrives in Dobbiaco at 9:35 am. To return, there is a 2:00 bus arriving in Cortina at 2:45 pm or a 3:10 bus arriving at 3:55 pm.

5. Sesto/Sexten Dolomites National Park (Parco Naturale Dolomiti di Sesto) - The park is a mountain hiker's dream—its irregularly shaped peaks and quiet valleys make this rugged, remote area a place of exceptional beauty, and the surrounding valleys are home to tiny, gleaming Südtirolean villages. The park covers 28,750 acres (11,635 hectares) around Dobbiaco/Toblach, San Candido/Innichen and Sesto/Sexten. Early astronomers used the park's densely packed peaks for orientation, and these summits were once referred to as "the world's most impressive sundial." During World War I, over 10,000 soldiers fought in these mountains as Austrian Tyroleans tried to defend themselves against invading Italians. Victims of this fighting are buried in a military cemetery in the Höhlenstein Valley, and there is a Peace Trail (Via della Pace/Friedensweg) on Monte Piano and on Mt. Fanes as a memorial to the horrors of war.

Directions: By car - Drive 30 miles northeast of Cortina. Reverse directions to return.

6. San Candido/Innichen - Lying east of Dobbiaco/Toblach at the entrance to the Val di Sesto, set in larch and pine forests, the small village of San Candido is home to the **Museo della Collegiata**, considered the Südtirol's most important Romanesque building. The **Monastery**, founded in 769, was replaced in 1170—with other parts of the church dating from the 12th to the 14th centuries. Note the monumental wooden statues, carved in the early 13th century. You may enoy taking the cable car in Vierschach, just east of San Candido/Innichen. It rises up to the Hahnspiel Hut at 6726 ft. (2050 m.).

Directions: By car - 51 north to Dobbiaco/Toblach, picking up 49 east into San Candido. Reverse directions to return.

7. Sesto/Sexten - A quiet, charming Tyrolean village with a population of only 1800, Sesto has only a few hotels, but is proud of its many flower-bedecked *pensioni*. Rudolf

Stolz, a local painter (1874 - 1960), lived in Sesto and his home is now a museum. The Monte Elmo lift in Sesto offers panoramas of the surrounding Sesto mountains. Or, walk to Moso/Moos, a neighboring village, and take the cable car up to the Rotwand Meadow at 6316 ft. (1925 m.). The scenery around and between Sesto and Moso is considered to be some of the most beautiful in the Dolomite valleys.

Directions: By car - 51 north to Dobbiaco. Drive east on 49 to San Candido and 52 south to Sesto and Moos. Reverse directions to return.

8. Bressanone/Brixen - See the "Selva/Wolkenstein" chapter, Excursion #4.

Directions: By car - 51 north from Cortina to Dobbiaco, picking up 49 west and south to Bressanone/Brixen. Reverse directions to return.

9. Venice - See the "Venice" chapter for details.

Directions: By car - 51 south, through Belluno. North of Belluno pick up *autostrada* A27 into Mestre and Venice. You'll go over a long causeway and arrive at a busy and confusing area, the Piazza Roma, a dead-end for car traffic. On your right is a pair of large, eight-story garages where you can park your car. There can be a long line of cars trying to get into these garages if you don't arrive by 9:00 am. Walk from the garage across the top of Piazza Roma to the Grand Canal piers and take the large, inexpensive, public water bus or Vaporetto to the San Marco stop. Reverse directions to return.

10. Innsbruck, Austria - See the chapter on "Selva/Wolkenstein," Excursion #10.

Directions: By car - 51 north to 49 west and pick up the *autostrada* A22 at the Brixen-Pustertal entrance. Drive north through the Brenner Pass, following directions to Innsbruck. Reverse directions to return. **Remember, if you leave Italy, take your passport!**

11. Chiusa/Klausen - See the "Merano" chapter, Excursion #10.

Directions: By car - 51 north to 49 west, picking up 12 south near Brixen into Chiusa. Reverse directions to return, or for a circle route, take 12 south and pick up 242 east through Ortesei and Selva, to 48 east. Drive over the Passo Sella, the Passo Pordoi and the Passo di Falzarego into Cortina. This is a magnificent drive back along the Dolomite Road but much slower because of all the hairpin turns on the mountain passes.

12. Brunico/Bruneck - This main town in the Puster Valley at 2805 ft. (858 m.) was founded in 1251 by the Bishop of Brixen. Fortification of the town was completed in the 14th century and remnants of these walls are still visible today. The medieval quarter is just below the 13th-century **Bishop's Castle**. On Stadtgasse, the old main street, visit the **City Apothecary** with its vaulted rooms, frescoes and coats of arms. Northwest of the St. Ursula Gate is the Baroque **Church of St. Ursula**, completed in the 1500s and renovated in Gothic style in the late 1800s. Just above where the Ahrn and Rienz Rivers meet is Brunico's Stegen district and the **Parish Church of St. Nicholas** with paintings from the 1400s. The **Bolzano Ethnographic Museum (Museo degli Usi e Costumi della Provincia di Bolzano)** now occupies the quarters of the courtier Mayr, and recreates a typical local village built around a 300-year-old mansion. It is open from Tuesday to Saturday, 9:30 am to 5:30 pm and Sunday from 2:00 to 6:00 pm.

Directions: By car - 51 north to 49 west and follow the signs for the local road into town. Reverse directions to return.

13. Lienz, Austria - Lienz, the main town in the eastern Tyrol district of Austria, lies in the shadow of the Dolomites and was cut off from the main part of the Tyrolean province when the Puster Valley (in the Südtirol) was transfered to Italy in 1919. Pay a visit to **Bruck Castle (Schloss Bruck)** and the **Museum of East Tyrol (Osttiroler Heimatmuseum)**. The castle was a fortress and now houses this museum with its collections of local antiquities, folklore and handiwork. The Knights' Hall is a good example of how the castle appeared in medieval times. The **Albin Egger-Lienz** gallery offers paintings of a local artist (1868-1926) whose work was often inspired by the Tyrol and its inhabitants. **St. Andrew's Church (St. Andrä)** is noted for its Gothic nave, but during restoration in 1968, murals from the 14th to the 17th centuries were uncovered. Under the gallery are the 16th-century Salzburg marble tombs of local nobility.

Directions: By car - 57 north to Dobbiaco, picking up 49 east over the Austrian border, becoming 100, into Lienz. Reverse directions to return. **Remember your passport!**

14. Belluno - With the Dolomites to the north and the Belluno Pre-Alps to the south, the city of Belluno developed on a rocky rise where the Piave and Ardo Rivers meet, its foundations on an ancient Roman settlement. The heart of the "old town" is made up of Renaissance-age streets, and when you walk in the Piazza del Duomo, the **Palazzo dei Rettori Veneziani** stands out; it is currently the headquarters of the Prefect. On its left is the old **Bishop's Palace**.

The southern side of the square is dominated by the majestic **Cathedral (Duomo)**, built in the 16th century. Note the beautiful paintings and the crypt, illuminated by four large windows facing in the direction of the Valle del Pieve. Next to the Duomo rises one of the most elegant Baroque **Towers** in Italy, created in 1743. The town center is closed at its southern end by **Porta Rugo**, with its original structures dating back to the 12th century, among streets and houses preserving the aura of medieval Belluno. Don't miss the cobblestone Via de S. Maria dei Battuti with its square and the **Church of San Pietro**, rebuilt in the 1700s on the foundations of the existing medieval church. Inside are two large, wooden altarpieces considered to be important works of art. Between the small Piazzetta delle Erbe and Piazza del Duomo is the 18th-century **Palazzo dei Giuristi** and the headquarters of the **Museo Civico** with exhibits of Venetian and Roman archeological finds.

Directions: By car - Follow signs to Venice, then local signs to Belluno. By bus - The 7:50 bus from Cortina arrives in Belluno at 9:50 am. To return, the 1:15 bus arrives at 3:00 pm and the 4:35 bus arrives in Cortina at 6:45 pm—via Alleghe and Agordo and an interesting drive through the Agordine Valley.

15. Lake Misurina - At 5761 ft. (1756 m.), Lake Misurina is one of the oldest known mountain resorts in the Dolomites. It is a small lake, circled by mountains, from Sorapis with its tiny glacier to the Marmarole, Cristallo and Cadini. On the north side, the celebrated Tre Cime di Lavaredo can be seen. Take the chairlift at the edge of the lake for spectacular views. (See Walks #2 and #5 for more details.)

Directions: By car - Follow signs in Cortina to Misurina, about a 20-minute drive. Reverse directions to return.

16. Bus Tours - Various travel companies in Cortina organize bus excursions. Check the back of the Cortina bus schedule for information. In the summer of 1994, there were bus excursions to Monte Piana, Croda da Lago, Lienz, Krimml Waterfalls, Venice, Südtirol castles, Salzburg, Val d'Isarco.

Cortina d'Ampezzo Walks

Recommended Maps:

1) Tabacco Carta Topografica - Cortina d'Ampezzo e Dolomiti Ampezzane - #03

2) Tabacco Carta Topografica - Dolomiti de Sesto/Sextener Dolomiten - #010

Walk #1: Introductory Walk along the Passeggiata

Walking Easy Time
2 to 4 hours

This gentle walk can be taken on the afternoon of arrival and is a good introduction to the immediate environs around Cortina. It is on the paved path, *passeggiata*, numbered 208 on Cortina d'Ampezzo hiking map "Tabacco - #03." The path, reserved for walkers only, runs north/south through Cortina and the Ampezzo Valley, past the hamlet of Zuel at 3809 ft. (1161 m.), with views of Tofana to the west, Sorapis to the east and Cristallo to the north—three of the famous Dolomite mountains surrounding the Ampezzo Valley. *Easy Walkers* will be hiking on trails in and around these mountains and valleys during their Cortina sojourn.

Start: Walk on the pedestrian street, and at the bust of Angelo Dibona at the bell tower next to the church, turn right or left and walk around and up the street, past the Hotel Ampezzo, crossing the main auto road. Turn right and pass the Faloria lift station (which you will be using this week) and continue onto the paved path reserved for walkers.

Enter the path and walk south to Zuel—crossing the auto road before reaching Zuel and then picking up the walking path again. Return on the same path, now walking north, with views of the dramatic Pomagagnon range and towering Cristallo. The round-trip from Cortina to Zuel is about one and one-half hours. If you wish, continue past the Faloria chairlift station, walking through the bus parking area for a short while, then pick up the paved *passeggiata* again to the north. This path continues further north for as far as you wish to walk. When you are ready, return to Cortina and visit the Church, the museums and shops, and the Tourist Office.

Walk #2: Rif. Auronzo to Rif. Lavaredo to Rif. Tre Cimi Locatelli/Drei Zinnen Hütte and Return

Walking Easy Time
3¾ hours

Today's walk is a "must do!" and it is suggested that *Easy Walkers* make this their first extended walk in the Cortina area. Make sure to leave an entire day for this hike—you will enjoy full exposure to the grandeur of the Dolomites. The day begins with a bus or auto ride over the gentle Tre Croce Pass in the direction of Lake Misurina, for a 21-mile (34-km) ride to Auronzo at 7540 ft. (2298 m.). This popular walk proceeds to circle the Tre Cimi (Three Chimneys), one of the best-known, most dramatic formations in the Dolomites. *Easy Walkers* will also visit the Rif. Lavaredo at 7691 ft. (2344 m.) and climb gently to a scenic viewpoint that will make you feel as if you stepped into the pages of a fairy tale about a magic mountain kingdom.

After recovering from the impact of this remarkable natural phenomenon, you will proceed towards your next destination for rest and repast at the Rifugio Locatelli/Drei Zinnen Hütte at 7891 ft. (2405 m.). If you look carefully along the way you will see the scars of a World War I battleground involving mountain troops of Italy and Austria. The *rifugio* will be filled with hikers who have come from around the world for the best views of these deeply crevassed "pale mountains." As the sun moves across the sky, the colors change, the shadows deepen—a kaleidoscope in slow motion. The walks ends with a return over the same trail, back to Aurenzo and your car or bus.

Directions: In Cortina and later, while driving over the Tre Croce Pass, follow signs towards Misurina. After passing lovely Lake Misurina, a sign will direct you to the right to Auronzo. Pay a local toll of 20,000 lire, and drive up to Rifugio Auronzo, where the walk begins. On busy summer days, parking attendants will direct you into an available spot. If you prefer to take the bus, there are 8:45 and 10:05 am buses from Cortina, arriving in Tre Cime at 9:45 am and 11:05 am. To return, buses leave Tre Cime at 3:00 and 4:40 pm, and arrive in Cortina at 3:55 and 5:45 pm.

Start: Where you park will determine how you access the well-engineered path towards Rifugio Laveredo. If you arrive early and are fortunate enough to park at a level close to Rifugio Auranzo, walk to the *rifugio*, picking up the wide path numbered 101-104. If the lower parking is filled, you will be directed higher up and closer to the dramatic Tre Cimi. You may then enter the wide path below by descending on a narrow trail meeting the main path. This is probably one of the most widely used trails in the Dolomites, and you'll have lots of company on today's hike.

As you walk towards the Rifugio Laveredo and its sun terrace, hold some enthusiasm in reserve, as this is only the beginning of one of the finest scenic hikes in the alps. On the left is the famous Tre Cime (Three Chimneys), and when bathed in sunlight, its pastel colors are revealed, depending on the sun's position and time of day. Just before Rif. Laveredo at 6705 ft. (2044 m.), the path forks, with #101 going steeply up to the left. Walk straight ahead on main path #104, past Rifugio Laveredo.

After a while the wide path narrows and you will follow the sign up to the Rifugio Locatelli, reaching the Paternsattel at 8052 ft. (2454 m.) in about a half hour, for a spectacular view of the Dolomites not seen earlier. Off to the far right is the Rif. Locatelli/Drei-Zinnen-Hütte, your destination. You will note however, that there are two paths visible in the direction of the *rifugio*. *Easy Walkers* will take the lower, wider path in preference to the narrow, hillside trail above, for the one-hour walk As you get closer to the *rifugio*, there is a narrow trail ascending steeply up to the right, blazed red and white, but continue on the main path, eventually walking up and around to the right.

The hike from the parking lot to the *rifugio* is about two hours. If you've packed lunch, there are many picnic opportunities in the area. After resting and taking in the outstanding scenery, return on the same path. On the drive back to Cortina, you might enjoy a stop at beautiful Lake Misurina, ringed by pine forests. (See Walk #5 for more details.)

Walk #3: Cortina Triple Lift to Tofana di Mezzo, Walk Col Druscie to Rifugio Ghedina to Cortina

Walking Easy Time
2½ hours

A triple cable car lift from 4019 ft. (1225 m.) to Tofana at 10,644 ft. (3244 m.) is the beginning of your excursion to one the locations used in Sylvester Stallone's "Cliff-hanger" movie. Remember that this excursion can be fully enjoyed only on a clear day. At the top station you will arrive at a large sun terrace for extensive views of the Dolomites surrounding Cortina d'Ampezzo. For those who wish, there is the opportunity to ascend several flights of steps to the walking paths along the peak at Tofana.

This is a rugged mountain and the peak should be visited only if you don't mind the high altitude and narrow paths. The peak is a popular starting place for serious rock climbers, and you may have the opportunity of watching them prepare to disappear over the cliff on hair-raising *ferrata* or iron-assisted expeditions to other Tofane locations. Plan to spend at least one hour on Tofana in order to absorb the remarkable visual impact of this stark, mountain wilderness.

You will take two sections of the lift down to Col Druscie at 5837 ft. (1779 m.), where the walk to Cortina begins, by way of the Rifugio Ghedina. For those who wish to return to Cortina more quickly, there is a walk down a ski run, taking you back to Cortina in one and one-half hours.

Directions: The Tofana lift is an easy 20-minute walk from the church in Cortina, past the ice rink, and while there is ample parking at the lift station, it is much easier to not drive through busy Cortina. Walk past the church on the pedestrian street and follow the signs to the ice rink and the Tofana Lift. Purchase a round-trip ticket to the top station, Tofana, which involves three cable cars. The first stop is Col Druscie, the next is Ra Valles, and the last one is at Tofana.

Start: After taking the three cable car rides to your final destination at Tofana, walk onto the large terrace for views of the Ampezzo Valley and the major peaks of the Dolomites and, on a clear day, as far as the Höhe Tauern in Austria. Take the steps in back of the terrace up to the engineered paths along the ridges of the Tofana peak. Guide ropes are provided as a precaution for walkers who want to enjoy the thrill of getting as close to the peak as possible. The views are remarkable, and you will probably see serious mountain climbers preparing for descents over the jagged ridge. Take the time necessary to absorb this one-of-a-kind panorama.

> ☞ **HINT:** *Easy Walkers* **who are not happy at great heights or who may be affected by the altitude, should enjoy this part of the excursion at the sun terrace and not attempt the narrow paths on Tofana.**

When ready, return to the first lift station at Col Druscie for the continuation of the walk. At the rear of the Col Druscie lift station is a large sign pointing right in the direction of Cortina. Walk to the right, descending easily on a grassy meadow, part of a ski run. The grassy path turns sharply right at 5512 ft. (1680 m.), but *Easy Walkers* will turn sharply left up a forest path for a short ascent, turning right on the jeep road numbered #409 and #410 on your map. Continue on, bearing right at the first intersection, and snake down the mountain to the auto road, where you turn right again, following the sign to the Rifugio Ghedina.

When you leave the *rifugio*, turn right on the road for a pleasant walk through the forest to a four-way auto intersection. Turn left on the lower left paved road (still #414) and descend to the main road where you will turn left for a few meters and then right, just past a bus stop, on a minor road that descends into Cortina. There are several options as you get close to Cortina. Take the routes that are less traveled, but keep descending with the church as your guiding beacon.

Walk #4: Cortina Lift to Faloria, Walk to Ristorante Rio Gere (Optional Excursion to Cristallo) to Rifugio Mietres to Rifugio Tondo to Cortina

Walking Easy Time
3½ hours

Today you will take the double cable car from Cortina to the top station at Rifugio Faloria, 6966 ft. (2123 m.). The second part of this ride is a breathtaking ascent to Faloria, high over deeply crevassed peaks. Walkers can continue on a steep, wide trail up to Rifugio Tondi at 7635 ft. (2327 m.) or take a private jeep at Faloria for the ride up to the top and additional, spectacular views from Tondi. You will walk down from Rifugio Faloria to Ristorante Rio Gere at 5571 ft. (1698 m.) on a gently descending, wide jeep road and continue through the forest to Rifugio Mietres at 5611 ft. (1710 m.) with its incredible views of the dramatic Pomagagnon range. The walk continues through the forest down to Rifugio Tondo at 4689 ft. (1429 m.). There is an option at Mietres to take one or two chairlifts between Mietres and Tondo for the continuation of the walk into Cortina.

Directions: At the bust of famed guide Angelo Dibona in front of the bell tower at the church, turn right or left and walk up and around to the main thoroughfare, passing the Hotel Ampezzo on your left and crossing the main auto road to the Faloria lift station on the right. Purchase a ticket to the top station, transferring to the waiting cable car at the mid-station. Cable cars run every half hour on the hour.

Start: The walk begins as you leave the cable car at Faloria at 6966 ft. (2123 m.). There is a large restaurant with sun terrace and facilities at the top station. *Easy Walkers*

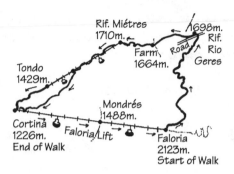

have an option here before to-day's itinerary begins. You can walk up the mountain to Rifugio Tondi at 7635 ft. (2327 m.), along a rocky, wide jeep path for outstanding views of the Dolomites on the other side of Faloria, returning to Faloria when ready. Or, if you don't wish to make the climb of almost 700 ft. (200 m.) but would like to visit Tondi, there is a private jeep taxi that will take you and bring you back from the peak for a reasonable fee.

The walk begins to the left, as you exit the lift station, on an **unsigned** wide, jeep road (#212), in the direction of Rio Gere. This is a one-hour, gentle, descending walk through the forest to the Ristorante Rio Gere, located on the main auto road to Cortina, next to the Cristallo chairlift. If the weather is clear, take the single chairlift to Son Forca at 7267 ft. (2215 m.) at the base of Cristallo, transferring to the gondola for the breathtaking ride to Rifugio Lorenzi at 9620 ft. (2932 m.)—the start of serious climbing expeditions over these jagged peaks and another "Cliffhanger" movie location. There are no hikes up here for *Easy Walkers*.

When ready, return to the base station next to the Rio Gere restaurant, where the walk continues. Walk down the auto road for a few meters and on the right, enter a grassy **unmarked** path paralleling the auto road off to the left. This unmarked path begins on the auto road between two white rocks, with a small wooden shrine (cross) at the beginning of the trail. After about 20 minutes, this path ends at a gravel road. Turn right and walk between the farmhouse and the barn at Malga de Larieto at 5460 ft. (1664 m.), **unsigned** but on your map. The path ascends gently towards Mietres at 5611 ft. (1710 m.). At a sign to Mietres, turn sharply left on a narrow, mountain trail. This gentle trail is usually wet and muddy going through the forest, so please be careful. Within a few minutes you will leave the forest and enter a meadow with the sun terrace of Rifugio Mietres framed by the jagged peaks of the Pomagagnon group—one of the most dramatic sites in the Cortina area.

After rest and repast, *Easy Walkers* have a number of options. You can walk down to Cortina in one and one-half hours, or take one or both of the single chairlifts that descend from Mietres to Col Tondo at 4689 ft. (1429 m.), with an easy walk back to Cortina. Or, you can walk down a grassy ski slope past Mietres to the jeep road, all the way to Tondo and into Cortina. At Col Tondo, follow the descending paved road back towards the church steeple in Cortina.

Walk #5: Lake Misurina Lift to Col de Varda, Rif. Citta di Carpi and Return, Lake Misurina circle

Walking Easy Time
3½ to 4 hours

Easy Walkers will drive to Lago di Misurina and the Col de Varda Lift Station, taking the chairlift (*seggovia*) to Col de Varda at 6939 ft. (2115 m.). The one and one-half hour walk to Rifugio Citta di Carpi is partly on a nicely graded trail that descends to 6473 ft. (1973 m.) with outstanding views of Cristallo, Sorapis, Tre Cimi and the Cadin di Misurina above you. The path continues on an ascending mountain trail that is well-blazed and easy to follow—from a low of 6375 ft. (1943 m.) to a final, short ascent to Rifugio Citta di Carpi at 6923 ft. (2110 m.).

Rif. Citta di Carpi welcomes picnickers on its outside tables, and after lunch and mountain viewing, you will return to the Col de Varda lift station along the same path. This walk, plus an hour's rest at the *rifugio*, will take about four hours round-trip. On your return to the base station, a gentle one-hour ramble around Lake Misurina provides a different perspective of the surrounding mountains. On the way back,

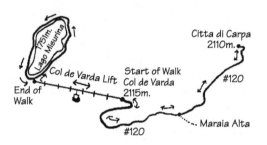

you might stop at the restaurant at Lago Scin, above Cortina, before the Cristallo lift, for cappuccino and fruit torte.

Directions: Leave Cortina by car for the 30-minute drive over the gentle Passo Tre Croce, following signs to Misurina. Just before the lake, turn right, following the sign to the Seggovia Col de Varde parking area. If you prefer to take the bus to Misurina, there is a 10:05 bus from Cortina, arriving in Misurina at 10:40 am. To return to Cortina, there is a 3:20 bus arriving 3:55 pm and a 5:10 bus arriving at 5:45 pm. Purchase a round-trip ticket for the single-person chairlift and the 12-minute ride to the top station.

Start: There are several signs at the back of the top station. Follow the sign on the tree to Citta di Carpi, #120 on your map, walking straight ahead on a wide path which turns down to the right and around the mountain, descending for an easy walk to 6375 ft. (1943 m.). The rugged Cristallo is in full view on your right, the massive Sorapis group across the valley ahead, and the jagged peaks of the Cadin are above you. Hopefully, you've picked a clear day for this hike.

The path splits and you will continue to walk straight ahead following the sign to Citta di Carpi, ascending on a mountain trail through the forest to 6893 ft. (2101 m.), then hiking up to your left to 6923 ft. (2110 m.) and the welcoming Italian flag flying above the *rifugio*. The level of ascent steepens on the last part of the hike—take it slowly but steadily and rest as often as needed.

The small *rifugio* welcomes walkers to use their outside tables and benches for picnics, inside is a restaurant serving local specialties, and facilities. When ready, return to Col de Varda along the same path, remembering that your initial descent is now an ascent. Descend on the chairlift to Lago di Misurina and take the pleasant, less than one-hour walk around the lake for additional views of the surrounding Dolomites before returning to your car and driving to Cortina or catching the late afternoon bus.

Walk #6: Cinque Torri Lift to Rif. Scoiattoli, Walk to Rif. Averau to Rif. Cinque Torri to Rif. Bái de Dónes at Base Station Cinque Torri Lift

Walking Easy Time
3 to 3½ hours

Plan the better part of the day for today's hike as you will want to spend extra time on this mountain watching climbers scale the famous Cinque Torri peaks. The Cinque Torri lift is on the Passo Falzarego road, a 20-minute drive from Cortina. The chairlift ascends from 6198 ft. (1889 m.), at its base station on the pass, to 6644 ft. (2025 m.) at the Rifugio Scoiattoli. Here you'll find new views of Tofana across the valley and the incredible five towers of Cinque Torri a few minutes walk from the sun terrace. You can walk up to the foot of Cinque Torri and watch climbers scaling the vertical faces of these rugged peaks. This area is a favorite training ground for climbers, from beginner to expert, and if you are interested, you might contact Mr. Giorgio Peretti at the Gruppo Guide Alpine Cortina (tel: 436-4740).

The walk begins back at the *rifugio* at the top station of the chairlift and ascends to Rifugio Averau's restaurant and facilities at 7917 ft. (2413 m.) on a wide path that becomes steeper towards the *rifugio*. At this altitude there are no trees or grass, only barren, rocky terrain, but the views from the terrace at Averau are worth the 1273 ft. (388 m.) climb. The walk continues down to the Rifugio Cinque Torri and then down the mountain along the road and through the forest on a mountain trail, to the Cinque Torri/Bái de Dónes chairlift base station and your car.

Directions: Driving from Cortina, follow the signs to Passo Falzerago, through the charming village of Pocol, for the 20-minute drive to the Cinque Torri Lift. Turn left into the large parking area at the sign "5 Torri Parking." Buy a one-way ticket to the top on the single chairlift for the 13-minute ride.

Start: The walk begins at the Rifugio Scoiattoli at 7300 ft. (2225 m.) with restaurant, sun terrace and facilities. Before starting, to observe the mountain climbers in action you should walk to the left on one of the little trails going up to the base of the Cinque Torri peaks. Athletes of all ages and both sexes climb the sheer faces of Cinque Torri at various levels of proficiency, and it is remarkable to see how quickly and efficiently they scale the peaks. You will probably spend about an hour taking in the action.

Return to the Rifugio Scoiattoli and proceed up the hill to the Rifugio Averau at 7917 ft. (2413 m.), sitting up on the mountain ridge in front of you. The wide path is rocky, devoid of any vegetation, and becomes steeper towards the *rifugio*. Take it slowly and reap the rewards of panoramic vistas at the top.

Come back on the same path towards Rif. Scoiattoli, but turn right on the wide, descending path just before the *rifugio* to the **unsigned** trail leading to Rifugio Cinque Torri, down on the right at 7012 ft. (2137 m.) with restaurant and facilities. This comfortable path gives you additional views of the climbers on Cinque Torri, now on the left.

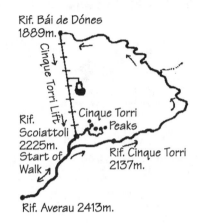

Walk past the *rifugio* on the rarely used auto road, following the sign to Rifugio Bái de Dónes, down and around the other side of Cinque Torri. After 15 to 20 minutes, depart from the road and into the forest at the sign to the left for Rifugio Bái de Dónes/Seggovia. This narrow forest trail descends for another 30 to 40 minutes to the parking area at the Cinque Torri lift.

Before returning to Cortina, you might wish to stop at the pretty little hamlet of Pocol, situated at 5020 ft. (1530 m.) on the Passo Falzerago, 3 miles (5 km) before Cortina. Park near the two large hotels, just off the road. Enjoy a visit to the popular "Pista Bar," before and to the rear of the Hotel Argentina. It is set on the side of a large, tranquil meadow filled with sun chairs and tables, a great place to relax with a cappuccino or a cold drink. Walk past the Hotel Argentina and the Hotel Tofana and turn left, following the sign "Belevedere" to a great viewpoint overlooking Cortina and the Ampezzo Valley. Further up the road is the Sacrario, a monument to peace where 10,000 solders who fought in World War I are buried. When ready, continue driving to Cortina d'Ampezzo.

Walk #7: Lagazuoi Lift to Rifugio Lagazuoi, Walk to Rifugio Scotoni to Cabin Alpina with Private Bus or Jeep Back to Lagazuoi Lift Base Station

Walking Easy Time
4 hours

This walk starts at a higher level than any of the other hikes in the Cortina area. It was suggested by Giorgio Peretti of the Gruppo Guide Alpine Cortina. The authors however, did not have the opportunity to take this hike.

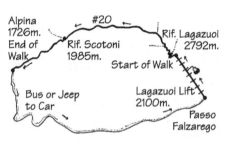

Leave Cortina on the Passo Falzarego road for the 30-minute drive to the Lagazuoi Lift Station at Passo Falzarego at 6890 ft. (2100 m.). Purchase a one-way cable car ticket to Rif. Lagazuoi at 9161 ft. (2792 m.), perched high on barren, rocky terrain, with a large, comfortable restaurant and sun terrace. Walk down trail #20 descending steeply at first, to Rif. Scotoni at 6513 ft. (1985 m.) for a descent of 2651 ft. (808 m.). This trail goes along the Alta Via Dolomiti and continues on trail #20 to Cabin Alpina at 5663 ft. (1726 m.). There is private van bus or jeep service to take walkers down to the road and back to the Lagazuoi parking area at the base station.

 HINT: Confirm the availability of the private bus service at Cabin Alpina with the Tourist Office before taking this hike. Service is usually available in July and August.

VIGO DI FASSA

Val di Fassa, rising from Moena at 3885 ft. (1184 m.) to Canazei at 4807 ft. (1465 m.), is one of the Dolomite valleys where the Ladin culture and language are still preserved, as well as elements of the Austrian character of the nearby Südtirol.

The small country villages of the Fassa valley are dwarfed and dominated by the high peaks of the Dolomite mountain ranges of Catinaccio and Latemar. These friendly villages attract winter sports enthusiasts and summer hikers who take advantage of the large network of cable cars, gondolas and chairlifts that criss-cross the mountains, meadows and valleys. Charming *ristorantes* and comfortable *rifugios*, situated along a myriad of trails, provide sun terraces with extraordinary views and mouth-watering, local menu specialties, adding extra incentives and additional dimensions to the days' activities.

Vigo di Fassa offers modern facilities that exist in harmony with its traditional history. Located midway between Canazei and Moena, Vigo was chosen as a *Walking Easy* base village as it is well-located for easy access to the area's hikes and because it is on an open, quiet, green hillside, away from the main auto road that bisects the valley. A major cable car in the center of Vigo rises to Ciampedie at 6555 ft. (1998 m.), the start of several *Easy Walker* hikes.

Campitello, a few kilometers to the north, has one of the largest cable cars in the Italian Alps, with the capacity to bring 130 passengers to Col Rodella at 7874 ft. (2400 m.) for additional hikes with unforgettable panoramas. Canazai provides lifts to Belvedere by way of Pecol for a famous hike to Passo Fedaia and Marmolada. A 20-minute drive through the Karer Pass/Passo Costalungo to the Rosengarten chair-lift near Lago di Carezza/Karersee takes walkers to more challenging hikes and close-up views of the Catinac-cio/Rosengarten range.

Local legend tells the following story of dwarf/magician King Laurin who owned a magificent rose garden. One day his enemies overwhelmed him and his empire disintegrated. He begrudged his enemies the splendour of his rose garden and he laid a curse on it—the roses were not to shine any more, neither by day nor by night. However, Laurin forgot the twilight, which is why today the Catinaccio/Rosengarten glows a magnificent rose color shortly before the sun sets.

In the Val di Fassa you will also have the opportunity of taking low-altitude walks through the valley on *passeggiate* and tasting *compagne cucina* (country cooking) at high-alti-tude *rifugios*. Store extra rolls of film in your backpack to capture the remarkable views and subtle colors of the Dolo-mites, especially at sunrise and sunset.

From Vigo di Fassa, travelers must pass through Ca-nazei, at the northern end of the Fassa Valley, in order to enter the Passo Pordoi. From here a twisting, mountain road heads to Arabba, Cortina d'Ampezzo, and south into the Agordino to such remote, scenic *Walking Easy* base villages as the lake town of Alleghe. Another sensational mountain auto road north of Canazei climbs over the Sella Pass with the majestic Sella mountain group on the right and the im-pressive Sassolungo on the left, snaking down to the tranquil Val Gardena (Gardena Valley) and Selva/Wolkenstein, an-other base village for *Easy Walkers*.

The Fassa Valley continues south from Canazei through the villages of Campitello, Pera di Sopra, Pozza di Fassa, Vigo di Fassa and the ancient town of Moena. Moena is the southern, commercial anchor to the valley and an important entrance to the San Pellegrino Pass for easy access to Falcade and on to the Agordine Valley. The inhabitants of the Val di Fassa hold a deep respect for their origins, honoring their Ladino identity, while at the same time, they work to meet the needs of the ever-growing numbers of tourists and walkers who come to this area each year.

Unlike Cortina d'Ampezzo with its sophisticated shops and clientele, the Val di Fassa attracts easy-going, casual Italian families for country vacations that include regional menu specialties, inexpensive wines, and many comfortable, family-owned, three-star hotels. The professionalism and efficiency of the innkeepers and local tourism directors and their staffs is highly impressive, and you will leave the valley with a strong feeling for the friendly villagers and their devotion to ensuring a warm and comfortable walking holiday.

There are many challenging hikes and remote *rifugios* in the Dolomites, and Vigo di Fassa and the Fassa Valley offer *Easy Walkers* a wide menu from which to choose a variety of day walks and excursions.

Transportation to Vigo di Fassa

By Air: The closest major international airports to Vigo di Fassa are in Munich, Germany, and Milan, Italy.

By Train: There are trains into Trento, Bolzano or Ora/Auer, and a bus then connects to Vigo di Fassa.

By Bus: Intercity coach service is available to Vigo di Fassa to and from Milan, Genoa, Bologna, Florence and Rome, and local bus service connects from Bolzano, Merano, Cortina d'Ampezzo, Trento and other cities, towns and villages in the Dolomites and South Tyrol regions. Buses run frequently in the Fassa Valley, with excellent service between Canazei and Moena and all the small villages in between, i.e., Vigo di Fassa, Pozza, Campitello, etc.

Sample Bus Timetables:

| Dep. Bolzano | 1:20 pm | 5:40pm |
| Arr. Vigo | 2:40 pm | 7:00 pm |

| Dep. Trento | 1:10 pm | 2:45 pm |
| Arr. Vigo | 3:24 pm | 4:59 pm |

By Car: If you fly into Milan and rent a car, pick up A4 *autostrada* north of the city, and drive east. After Lake Garda and before Verona, pick up *autostrada* A22 north and exit at Egna/Ora to pick up 48 east through Predazzo and Moena. Watch for the turn-off to Vigo di Fassa about three miles (5 km) past Moena.

If you fly into Munich, take *autobahn* A94 south to Garmisch-Partenkirchen, picking up 2 east and then 177 south to Innsbruck. Take the *autobahn* east and then cut south through the Brenner Pass to Italy where the road becomes *autostrada* A22 south. Exit at Egna/Ora and take 48 east into Vigo, watching for the turn-off about three miles (5 km) after Moena.

From Trento, Verona and the southern regions, leave the Brenner *autostrada* at the Egna/Neumarkt exit and take the S.S.48 delle Dolomiti road through Cavelese, Predazzo and north to Moena. About three miles (5 km) past Moena, watch for the left turn to Vigo di Fassa.

From the north on the Brenner Highway, exit at Bolzano Nord and follow signs to the Val d'Ega/Eggental (which begins on the east side of the *autostrada*). Drive southeast through this valley, staying left on 241, then over the Passo di Costalunga (Karer Pass) into Vigo.

From Venice, drive north through Belluno and take S203 to Agordo, turning left through the Passo S. Pellegrino, then turning right at Moena to Vigo di Fassa.

From the east and Cortina d'Ampezzo areas, drive west on 48 through the Passo di Falzarego and the Passo Pordoi, through Canazei, picking up the right turn to Vigo di Fassa just past Pozza di Fassa.

Excursions in and around Vigo di Fassa

This section introduces day excursions for *Easy Walkers* to enjoy when the weather is not suitable for high-altitude walking, or when an alternative to walking is desired. The helpful and multi-lingual Tourist Office in Vigo di Fassa is on the main street at Via Roma 18, in the center of town (tel: 64093). Be sure to check current timetables if using public transportation.

1. Lifts in and around Vigo di Fassa:

A) Funivia Catinaccio - A large cable car takes you to the top station of Ciampedie, with fabulous close-up views of the Catinaccio/Rosengarten. This lift is open from 8:30 am to 1:00 pm and 2:10 pm to 6:30 pm. (See Walks #3 and #5 for more details.)

B) Vajolet 1 and 2 - A double-stage chairlift rises from Pera, a few kilometers east of Vigo, to Ciampedie and Cigolade. It is open from 8:30 am to 12:20 pm and 2:00 pm to 5:30 pm.

2. Towns of the Val di Fassa - The Fassa Valley is 12½ miles (20 km) long, with about 8500 inhabitants living in its villages, at an average altitude of 4429 ft. (1350 m.). The seven villages of Vigo di Fassa, Pozza di Fassa, Soraga, Mazza, Moena, Campitello and Canazei make up the Val di Fassa, in the heart of the Trentino Dolomites and at the center of Italy's most famous mountain ranges: the Catinaccio/Rosengarten, Latemar, Marmolada, Monzini, Sassolungo, and the Sella.

A) Pozza di Fassa - Less than two miles (3 km) from Vigo, Pozza di Fassa is at the widest part of the valley and carries on the mountaineering tradition of this Dolomite region. One of the greatest climbers of all time, Tita Perez, "Devil of the Dolomites," was born outside of Pozza. The village is dominated by the peaks of the magnificent Cima Undici and Cima Dodici, and the meeting of the Avisio River with the stream of S. Nicole occurs on the outskirts of town. Nearby are areas of geological and mineralogical significance, including the ancient Monzoni range of mountains, a phenomonon dating back tens of millions of years.

Directions: By car - Drive east on the road out of town and turn left on the main road for the brief ride. By bus - There are frequent buses going to and coming from Pozza.

B) Soraga - Two and one-half miles (4 km) south of Vigo is Soraga, a tiny, tranquil village in magnificent surroundings. Near the village, on the right side of the Aviso River, the most ancient rocks of the Fassa Valley appear. The Soraga church was built in 1514, on the site of an even older church, but a flood in 1885 destroyed its ancient bell-tower.

Directions: By car - Drive east on the road out of town and turn right on the main road for the short ride. By bus - There are frequent buses going to and coming from Soraga.

C) Mazzin - This peaceful village, four and one-half miles north of Vigo, surrounded by spacious green fields, is the heart of the valley and an area where many high-altitude walks begin. The nearby Doss dei Pigui is an area of great archeological significance—major discoveries of prehistoric remains continue to be found there today. These relics can be seen in the local museum.

Directions: By car - Drive east on the road out of Vigo and turn left on the main road, driving past Pozza di Fassa and following the sign to Mazzin. By bus - There are frequent buses going to and coming from Mazzin.

D) Moena - Four and one-quarter miles (7 km) south of Vigo di Fassa, Moena, the largest town in the Val de Fassa with 2600 inhabitants, lies at an altitude of 3937 ft. (1200 m.). Moena treasures its Ladin culture and language, and in local legend, this village is the kingdom of mythical King Laurino and is called "Fairy of the Dolomites." At sunset, the surrounding mountains take on the fiery red hue made famous in photographs of the area. Enjoy the spectacular views of the Catinaccio and Sassolungo mountain ranges. Note the Roda di Vael stones silhouetted against the sky—use your imagination here to see a profile of legendary King Laurino.

While the village is an ideal starting point for many summer walks, it is also known for its elegant shops and chic boutiques. **Lusia** is a local two-section cable car and gondola lift, open from 9:00 am to 12:30 pm and 2:30 to 6:00 pm.

Directions: By car - Turn right on 48 for the ten-minute ride to Moena. By bus - There are many buses going to and coming from Moena.

E) Campitello - Situated six miles (10 km) north of Vigo, Campitello is dominated by the Col Rodella, forming a beautiful and natural balcony onto the Dolomites. This upper Fassa Valley village is the home of the Ciamorces, famous alpine guides who proudly boast of their mountaineering feats and countless daring rescue missions.

Campitello is also the site of one of the largest cable cars in the entire Italian Alps—the **Col Rodella**, which rises to panoramic views of Val di Fassa, Gruppo Sella and Sassolungo. It is open from 8:45 am to 12:30 pm and 2:00 pm to 6:00 pm. (See Walk #2.) The village of Campitello is tiny, with only 700 inhabitants—note the well-preserved old farmhouses in the hills surrounding the village.

Directions: By car - Turn left on the main road towards Canazei. By bus - There are many buses serving Campitello.

F) Canazei - Eight miles (13 km) north of Vigo, Canazei lies on the main Dolomite Road to the famous Sella, Pordoi and Fedaia Passes. It is close to the Marmolada Range, and you can drive east of the village for a superb view of this area, framed by the Catinaccio, the Towers of Vaioletto (Torri del Vaiolet), the Sella Massif and the Marmolada. Canazei is an enjoyable place to explore, with an interesting piazza, inviting shops and the intriguing architecture of its old buildings.

Lifts in Canazei include the **Pecol**, providing panoramic views of the Val di Fassa and the mountains surrounding Canazei (open from 8:45 am to 12:30 pm and 2:00 to 6:00 pm) and the gondola **Col dei Rossi**, an adjunct of the Pecol cable car, rising even higher for spectacular views (open from 8:45 am to 12:30 pm and 2:00 to 6:00 pm). (See Walk #6 for more details.)

Directions: By car - 48 north to Canazei. By bus - There are many buses going to and returning from Canazei.

G) S. Giovanni di Fassa - This tiny hamlet is located right below Vigo di Fassa and depends on Vigo for all its services. Its name derives from the Pieve di S. Giovanni, the largest religious and artistic monument in the Fassa Valley. The Gothic church was built in late 1400 on the site of an earlier church built about 1000. Each time the bell rings in this church, a legend is perpetuated. Supposedly in 1549, while the bell was being cast, a woman threw a bronze vessel full of precious metals, that her husband Soldà had stolen from the Turks, into the large melting pot. Soldà was going to kill his wife because of the lost treasure and because he felt the bell would be damaged. However, when the bell was cast the sound was perfect, and since then, every time the bell rings the villagers attribute its beautiful sound to the precious metal stolen from the Turks in the 16th century!

3. Bolzano/Bozen - See the "Selva/Wolkenstein" chapter, Excursion #3.

Directions: By car - Take 241 through the Passo di Costalunga (Karer Pass), through the Valle D'Ega (Eggental), following signs into Bolzano/Bozen. Reverse directions to return. By bus - The 8:45 bus arrives in Bolzano/Bozen at 10:05 am and the 5:40 bus arrives in Vigo at 7:00 pm.

4. Trento - Stop by the local Tourist Office and ask for the "Orientation Map of Trento," to be used during this one-day *Walking Easy* itinerary. See the chapter on "Baselga di Pinè," Excursion #8, for more details.

Directions: Trento is 56 miles (91 km) southwest of Vigo di Fassa. By car - Drive through Moena on 48, staying east on the road at Predazzo until you reach Ora/Auer where you pick up 12 south into Trento. Reverse directions to return. By bus - the 7:01 bus from Vigo arrives in Trento at 9:15 am, the 9:11 bus arrives at 11:25 am. To return, the 2:55 bus arrives in Vigo at 5:00 pm or the 6:30 bus arrives at 8:44 pm.

5. Cortina d'Ampezzo - See the "Cortina d'Ampezzo" chapter for more details.

Directions: By car - Drive north on 48 through Canazei, Passo Pordoi, and Passo Falzarego to Cortina. Reverse directions to return.

6. Merano/Meran - See the chapter on "Merano/Meran" for more details.

Directions: By car - Drive to the outskirts of Bolzano/Bozen and pick up 12 south. After a short drive, take 38 north into Merano. Reverse directions to return.

7. Rovereto - Second only to Trento in population and political importance, Rovereto is a medieval town with a 14th-century **Castle (Castello)** looming over its houses. The town's Venetian connections are still visible in the **Palazzo Municipale** and the **Church of San Marco**. During World War I, thousands of Italian and Austrian troops were killed in this area, and one of the largest bells in the world, the **Bell of the Fallen (Campana dei Caduti)** on nearby Miravelle hill, tolls one hundred times at sunset to eulogize victims around the world.

Directions: By car - Take 48 west to 12 south into Rovereto. Reverse directions to return.

8. Egna/Neumarkt - Egna is an ancient town south of Bolzano/Bozen, established in 1189 as a trading post. For centuries its craftsmen and merchants enjoyed trade between Germany and Italy. When the railroad was introduced into the area in the mid-1800s and bypassed the town, Egna/Neumarkt became a sleepy, rural backwater. However, its ancient arcades and narrow streets have been restored, and the **Museum for Common Culture** on Andreas-Hofer-Lauben 24 is an introduction to typical 19th-century lifestyles of this area along the Brenner Road.

Directions: By car - Drive on 241 to Bolzano/Bozen, not entering the A22 *autostrada*, but picking up 12 south to Egna/Neumarkt. Reverse directions to return. By bus - The 9:11 bus from Vigo arrives in Egna at 10:45 am. To return, the bus leaves Egna at 3:25 and arrives in Vigo at 5:00 pm.

9. Ortesei/St. Ulrich - See the "Selva/ Wolkenstein" chapter, Excursion #2.

Directions: By car - drive north past Canazei and pick up 242 north through the Passo Sella (Sellajoch). Drive past Selva/Wolkenstein, continuing on to Ortesei. Reverse directions to return.

10. Verona - See the "Baselga di Pinè" chapter, Excursion #9.

Directions: By car - Take 48 south to *autostrada* A22 south, then follow local signs into Verona. Reverse directions to return.

11. Venice - See our chapter on "Venice" for more details.

Directions: By car - 48 south to Predazzo, picking up 50 south, and then 50b west into 47 south. This will take you through Bassano to the outskirts of Padua, where you take E70 *autostrada* to Venice. You'll go over a long causeway and arrive at a busy and confusing area, the Piazza Roma, a dead-end for car traffic. On your right is a pair of large, eight-story garages where you can park your car. There can be a long line of cars trying to get into these garages if you don't arrive before 9:00 am. Walk from the garage across the top of Piazza Roma to the Grand Canal Piers and take the large, inexpensive, public water taxi or Vaporetto to San Marco. Reverse directions to return.

12. Padua - See the "Baselga di Pinè" chapter, Excursion #10.

Directions: By car - Follow 48 south to Predazzo and pick up 50 south, then 50b west to 47 south, through Bassano into Padua. Reverse directions to return.

13. Bressanone/Brixen - See the "Selva/ Wolkenstein" chapter, Excursion #4.

Directions: By car - 241 west to 12 north into Bressanone/Brixen. Reverse directions to return.

14. Falcade - The tiny village of Falcade lies at 3757 ft. (1145 m.) between the Pale di San Martino, the Civetta and Marmolada, a wonderful position for winter and summer sports activities. Boasting interesting old farmhouses and spectacular views of Mt. Civetta, Mt. Pelmo and the Pale di San Martino, Falcade extends along a sunny slope to the bottom of the valley, until it reaches the houses of Falcade Alto at 4255 ft. (1297m.). Visit the **Church of San Sebastiano** with its pointed bell tower and fine interior paintings. The village is internationally known in the world of modern art because of wood sculptors Dante Moro and Augusto Murer. Their studios are also art galleries, open to the public.

Directions: By car - Drive to Moena, turning southeast for 6 miles (10 km) over the San Pellegrino Pass to Falcade. Reverse directions to return.

15. Bus Tours - Excursions are available from Vigo di Fassa by local Atesina bus—current prices and timetables are available at the Tourist Office. Destinations include Innsbruck and Salzburg in Austria, Munich, Cortina d'Ampezzo, Lake Misurina, Corvara, Livigno, Brunico/Bressanone, Merano/Glorenza, Pietralla/Lago di Carezza and Passo Sella/Ortesei. **Remember, when leaving Italy, take your passport!**

Vigo di Fassa Walks

Recommended Maps:

1) Tabacco Carta Topografica #06 - Val di Fassa e Dolomiti Fassane

2) Val di Fassa - Passeggiate/Escursioni - Catinaccio, Sella, Marmolada, Monzoni

3) Vigo di Fassa, Pozza di Fassa - Local Map

4) Moena, Soraga - Local Map

5) Canazei - Local Map

Maps 2, 3, 4, and 5 are available free of charge from any local Val di Fassa Tourist Office.

Walk #1: Introductory Walk—Vigo di Fassa to Larzonei to Vallunga and Return

 Walking Easy Time
2 hours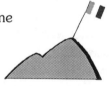

This walk can be clearly followed on the local map of Vigo di Fassa/Pozza di Fassa, available at the Tourist Office, and you might want to pick up this map before you begin. This short walk serves as an introduction to the lovely meadow and forest area south of Vigo di Fassa, and can be a good activity for your arrival afternoon. The walk begins at Vigo's village center and winds down through the meadows on a *passeggiata*, almost all the way to Tamion, then turns up through the forest to Vallunga and back to Vigo.

Start: Walk west through the village center along the road, crossing the auto road just past the "SPAR" market and entering onto the small street marked "Via Valle." Walk straight ahead on this picturesque, cobblestone street and at the second shrine on Via Belvedere, take the small, unpaved, middle path between two old, wooden barns. This path leads down the meadow to an unmarked *passeggiata*, where you bear right to the road into Larzonei. Follow the road around and pick up the signed path towards Tamion.

The path descends through the forest, crossing over the river on a narrow wooden bridge. Follow the sign to the right to Vallunga, as the path ascends up to 4964 ft. (1513 m.), for a rise of about 427 ft. (130 m.). This path crosses the stream again, bringing you out to the main auto road.

Cross the road and immediately take the ascending path up to the lovely old church, built in 1700 and dedicated to S. Giovanni Nepomuceno, located in the center of Vallunga. Make a right turn at the church and a left almost immediately, onto the walking path in the direction of Vigo di Fassa.

This gentle path descends to Vigo parallel to the auto road down on your right. Continue straight ahead in the signed direction of Vigo. Do **not** turn up to the left on a *passeggiata* in the direction of Vael. When the path ends, turn left on the main street for a walk through Vigo di Fassa.

Walk #2: Lift to Col Rodella, Walk to Rifugio Friedrich August to Rifugio S. Pertini to Malga Sasso Piatto to Rifugio Micheluzzi/Duron to Campitello

Walking Easy Time
4 hours

Reserve the better part of a clear day for this sensational hike. At Campitello you will take one of the largest cable cars in the alps, holding 130 people, for the ascent to Col Rodella at 7874 ft. (2400 m.) and spectacular views of the Sella group, Sassolungo, Sassopiatto, and Catinaccio.

The walk begins with a descent to the Rifugio August and continues along the base of the Sassolungo/Sassopiatto on the Friedrich Augustweg. This narrow, mountain-side trail, running between 7546 and 7874 ft. (2300 and 2400 m.), is mostly comfortable, but there are enough rocky scrambles to rate it "more challenging."

The views of the Dolomites are dazzling, and it is possible to cross over into the next valley, the Val Gardena, through Alpe di Siusi. Today, though, *Easy Walkers* will descend at the Malga del Sasso Piatto (dairy farm) through the valley, to the Rifugio Micheluzzi at 6103 ft. (1860 m.) for a view of one of the prettiest pastoral scenes in the Italian Alps. The hike ends with a walk down a traffic-free gravel road, all the way to Campitello and your car.

Directions: Drive to Campitello and park in the large parking area at the base station of the Funivia Col Rodella. Buy a one-way ticket to the top station and take the large, modern cable car for the seven-minute ride to Col Rodella at 7832 ft. (2387 m.).

Start: There is only one sign at the top, directing hikers up 328 ft. (100 m.) to the Rifugio Col Rodella at the peak to the left, but *Easy Walkers* will walk straight ahead, down to an intersection visible below, just before the Rifugio F. August. This is the starting point of several walks, and it is well signed. Walk left and ahead, following directions to Rif. F. August at 7540 ft. (2298 m.), and then to Rif. Sandro Pertini at 7546 ft. (2300 m.). The trail to Rif. Pertini is pleasant, fairly level, and well-traveled—a 45-minute walk with astounding views of the surrounding Dolomites.

On leaving Rif. Pertini, path #594 becomes a typical mountain *bergweg*, more challenging as it narrows, with a few rocky scrambles before descending to the small farm, Malga del Sasso Piatto, at 7376 ft. (2248 m.). The farm is reached by taking the **unsigned** mountain trail down to the left and splitting off the main trail **before** Rif. Sasso Piatto, visible up on the hillside. Towards the bottom of this descent, look for blue blazing and blue arrows on a huge boulder before the farm, directing you to the left on trail 533 to Rif.

Duron (called Micheluzzi on many maps).

This well-beaten, blazed trail descends on the meadows through the valley,

near a mountain stream, eventually turning and crossing it. The trail continues, steeply at times, into the forest and down to a country road. Cross the road, picking up the path again, and within a few minutes you will be at the Rif. Micheluzzi/Duron at 6103 ft. (1860 m.). It's okay to picnic here at the *rifugio*, providing you purchase your beverages inside.

☞ **HINT:** While there are picnic tables in front of the *rifugio*, walk around to the rear for additional tables and a scene you will always remember—herds of cows wandering through a large green meadow that reaches up to the jagged peaks of Denti di Terrarossa in the distance.

When ready to leave, walk up to the road and turn right for the descent all the way into Campitello. Walk down through Campitello on Via Rodella with the river on the right, and cross the auto road to the parking area at the cable car base station.

Walk #3: Catinaccio Cable Car to Rif. Ciampedie, Walk from Rif. Gardeccia (Optional walk to Rif. Vajolet and Return) to Pera di Sopra to Vigo di Fassa

Walking Easy Time
3¾ to 5¼ hours

Plan to take this high-level walk on a clear day, as the views of the jagged peaks of Catinaccio/Rosengarten are breathtaking. You will take the large cable car from Vigo di Fassa to Rifugio Ciampedie at 6552 ft. (1997 m.) where the walk begins. The path to Rifugio Gardeccia at 6398 ft. (1950 m.) is a popular, comfortable forest trail.

At Gardeccia you have the option of walking up to Rifugio Vajolet at 7359 ft. (2243 m.), and further into the Vajolet Valley, which ascends all the way to 8531 ft. (2600 m.). For those who do not wish to ascend the additional 961 ft. (293 m.) to Vajolet, the walk continues down along the side of a cobblestone road with fabulous views of the Catinaccio/Rosengarten above and the Sella group ahead. The road leads to the village of Pera di Sopra at the main road for the walk through Meida and Pozza to Vigo di Fassa. There is an option to take the bus from Pera to Vigo, depending on the time.

Directions: In Vigo, take the cable car at the Funivia Catinaccio/Seilbahn Rosengarten and buy a one-way ticket for the short ride to the top at Rifugio Ciampedie.

Start: Follow the sign "546 Vajolet." After a few minutes you will reach the Rifugio Negritella, where the path splits, 545 going down to Vigo by way of the Rif. Roda di Vael. Today, however, walk straight ahead, across a ski slope and under a ski lift, emerging from the forest at the Rif. Catinaccio. Walk around the *rifugio* to the open, grassy plateau and the Rifugios Gardeccia and Stella Alpina. Trail 546 continues up and past the Rifugio Vajolet which sits high on the mountain for those *Easy Walkers* who would like more of a challenge on today's itinerary. The wooden benches in the meadow can be a great place for a picnic.

At Gardeccia, walk down to the left of the *rifugio* to the **unmarked**, stone jeep road (marked 546 only on your map), with the river on the right and the soaring peaks of Catinaccio up on the left. You might

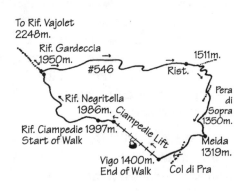

find it more comfortable walking on the small grassy strip alongside the cobblestone road. After about 40 minutes the road becomes paved, as you continue descending gently towards Pera, with impressive scenery in all directions. Stop at Restaurant La Regolina on the right, if a cappuccino break on the pretty sun terrace seems indicated.

Continue walking on the road until you come to a sign for the Regolina restaurant. You depart from the auto road here, descending to the right on a "chapel path" that winds down into Pera. Walk through Pera to the main auto road, past some old barns, the church and cemetery on Via Tita Piaz.

Turn right on the main road in the direction of Vigo. Just past the auto dealer, cross the road, and walk to the Hotel Christina. Walk past the hotel, crossing the meadow in back of the hotel gently to the right (in the two-o'clock direction), and walk over the bridge, on the path up and through the meadow to the little village of Meida. Enter the village on Via Laurino, making a right on Via Cavour, crossing the bridge and turning right immediately onto the *passieggiata*. In Pozza, cross another bridge to the right, then turn left and walk along the main road for a short time to Col da Prà, where you ascend to the main street in Vigo.

If you prefer to take the bus from Pera to Vigo, coming off the chapel trail instead of turning right onto Via Tita Piaz, turn left onto Via Catanaccio and walk to the main road and the bus stop, remembering that buses leave Pera for Vigo at 2:58, 3:33 and 5:20 pm on the Atesina line and 3:18 and 4:58 pm on the SAD line. (Check the bus schedules before taking today's walk.)

Walk #4: Chairlift Rosengarten to Rifugio Paolina to Monument Cristomannos with Return, to Base Station Rosengarten (Optional Excursion to Lake Carezza)

Walking Easy Time
3 hours

Today's walk begins at the Rosengarten/Catinaccio chairlift, a 20-minute drive over the Karerpass/Passo Costalunga, with a 15-minute, pleasant double chairlift glide over a golf course and green meadows to the Rifugio Paolina at 6972 ft. (2125 m.). There are several walks from this point, but *Easy Walkers* will walk up 735 ft. (224 m.) on a twisting mountain trail to Monument Cristomannos. Here you will find stunning panoramic views of the Latemar mountain group across the valley, with dramatic peaks just under 9900 ft. (3000 m.), the Catinaccio/Rosengarten group above you that rises to 9843 ft. (3000 m.) and the soft, green meadows and darker green forests below.

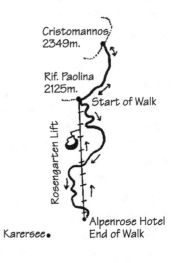

After returning to the lift station, you will walk down the mountain, on a zig-zagging, well-defined trail that can be steep at times, but not dangerous. This walk is rated "more challenging" because there is **no** level walking, only a steep ascent and a long descent. However, you have the option of returning to the base station by the same chairlift you came up on.

Directions: Leave from Vigo di Fassa on the main auto road through Vallonga and the Karerpass/Passo Costalunga, to the Rosengarten Chairlift on the right side of the road, with ample parking at the base station. Purchase a one-way ticket and board the double-seater chairlift for the 15-minute ride to the top station.

Start: At the top station, walk to the right of the Rifugio Paolina and follow one of several signs to Mon. Cristomannos. This highly visible, popular path up the mountain climbs to your destination under the peak of Roda di Vael. *Easy Walkers* may find the ascent steep, but it appears to be a cakewalk for most Europeans as the trail was filled with families—hikers from the ages of 2 to 80. Take the ascent slowly and enjoy the view at the monument, a large bronze eagle dedicated to Dr. Cristommanos of Merano who understood the importance of tourism in the area and proposed the now-famous Dolomite road.

Return to the Rifugio Paolina, the top station of the chairlift, and after perhaps a picnic or lunch at the *rifugio*, continue down on the path marked "Sesselift Tal Station" to the bottom of the chairlift and parking area. This trail zig-zags down the mountain to ease the level of descent, next to and under the chairlift, steeply at first, but it eases off nicely onto the meadow and through the golf course to a road that winds down to the parking area at the lift station. This part of the walk should take about one hour and fifteen minutes. Remember that walking downhill can bring stress to your knees—take small steps, keep your laces tight, and rest often.

If time permits, drive five minutes further west to Lago di Carezza, parking in a large lot on the right for a 1500-lire parking fee. Cross the road for a walk around the pretty little lake, through the Latemar forest. If you wish, you can walk on several small trails, off to the right of the main split-fence trail, that reach further up into the forest, where locals search for wild mushrooms, a favorite pastime in this area.

> ☞ **HINT: Caution! Check with experienced "mushroom people" before eating any mushrooms you pick!**

We've seen hikers come out of the forest with baskets of mushrooms, some as large as a foot across. However, there are strict regulations concerning the picking of mushrooms, i.e., weight, size, amount, etc., and a permit is necessary—

check with the Tourist Office. The walk around the lake takes about one-half hour on a pretty forest path and is a pleasant break in the day.

Walk #5: Catanaccio Lift to Ciampedie, Rifugio Negritella to Vigo di Fassa on the Alta Via di Fassa

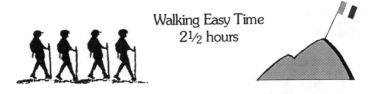

Walking Easy Time
2½ hours

Today's hike begins at the Rifugio Ciampedie at 6552 ft. (1997 m.), after ascending on the cable car from Vigo di Fassa. The path goes through the southern forest of Ciampedie, in the direction of the Rifugio Roda di Vael, and *Easy Walkers* may descend to Vigo on route 547 without having to ascend to the Rif. Vael, a climb of 886 ft. (270 m.).

Directions: Purchase a one-way ticket at the Funivia Catinaccio in Vigo for the quick cable car ride to Ciampedie.

Start: Walk to the Rif. Negritella and follow the sign for #545 Rif. Roda di Vael. This path is called the "Alta Via di Fassa/Fassaner Höhenweg" and winds around the mountain, with the usual ascents and

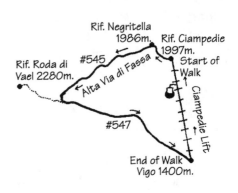

descents, to the Rif. Roda di Vael. After about one and one-half hours, and before the *rifugio*, you will meet another path. A walk to the right brings you up 886 ft. (270 m.) to the Rifugio Vael, but a left turn takes walkers down to Vigo di Fassa on #547, which meets a jeep road at 5013 ft. (1528 m.), taking you into Vigo di Fassa.

The following walks were suggested by the helpful personnel at the Tourist Office in Vigo di Fassa:

Walk #6: Canazei Lift to Pecol and Cable Car to Belvedere, Walk to Lago di Fedaia via the Bindelweg/Viel del Pan, Excursion to Marmolada

Walking Easy Time
$3\frac{1}{2}$ to 4 hours

This sensational walk, using lifts from Canazei, offers new views of Marmolada across the valley and above Lago di Fedaia. It will also be possible to take the standing, bucket chairlift at the reservoir for a visit to the glacier at Marmolada at 7304 ft. (2226 m.). Note the following important items:

1) It is essential to take the bus from the **Passo di Fedaia** side of the reservoir back to Canazei, which you can reach via the traffic-free road on the far side of the lake (a 30-minute walk). This bus usually operates during the months of June, July and August and the first ten days of September.

2) Check with the Vigo Tourist Office to make sure the bus is operating on the day you plan to take this hike, and ask for the afternoon bus schedule, ensuring you plan the day's activities accordingly.

3) The path down to Lago di Fedaia from the Bindelweg (the last 15 minutes of the hike), is on a steep, grassy slope and can be slippery. Take the descent slowly.

Directions: Purchase a one-way ticket at the Canazei lift to Pecol, continuing on the cable car to Col dei Rossi/Belvedere at 7819 ft. (2383 m.), where the walk begins.

Start: Walk down to the Rifugio Belvedere at 7671 ft. (2338 m.), then up to Rifugio Fredaroia at 7835 ft. (2388 m.). Proceed past Fredaroia to pick up route 601 to the right (Bindelweg) to Rifugio Viel del Pan at 7979 ft. (2432 m.). Continue all the way on 601, finally winding down to the reservoir, Lago di Fedaia, on a steep trail. This walk, with views of Marmolada and its glacier, should take *Easy Walkers* about 3 to 3½ hours.

Walk across the road and the reservoir and up to the little lift station for the standing, bucket lift ride up to 8616 ft. (2626 m.) at the leading edge of the glacier, the view you saw across the valley on the Bindelweg. This is a spectacular ride-try not to miss it!

☞ **HINT: The two-person, standing bucket lift requires some special attention when getting on and off. There are attendants who will help you. Move quickly and firmly and follow directions.**

After returning to the bottom lift station, walk down to the unused road and walk to the far end of the reservoir to the parking area at Passo di Fedaia for the bus return to Canazei.

Walk #7: Chairlift Rosengarten to Rifugio Paolina, Walk to Monument Cristomannos via the Hirzlweg to Paolina

Walking Easy Time
3 hours

This more challenging walk begins at Rifugio Paolina at 6972 ft. (2125 m.) after taking the Rosengarten Chairlift from 5315 ft. (1620 m.). This chairlift is reached by driving from Vigo di Fassa through the Karerpass/Passo Costalunga, to the location of the chairlift on the right, a few minutes before Lake Carezza/Karersee.

This popular path goes to the left on #552 from the Rif. Paolina, in the direction of the Rosengartenhütte/Rif. Coronelle, on a narrow, mountainside trail that can be slip-

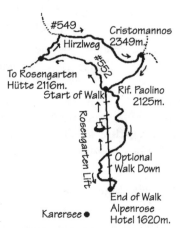

pery and rocky at times. After walking about 20 minutes, at a signed intersection at 6943 ft. (2116 m.), take the path turning sharply up the mountain to the right, in the direction of Cristomannos on #549, ascending to the monument at 7707 ft. (2349 m.). This is an ascent of 765 ft. (233 m.), most of which is done during the first and last part of the climb. The monument is dedicated to the doctor from Merano who first envi-

...e road through the Dolomites which opened this

...urism. The trail descends steeply to the Rif. Paolina,

where there are two options. If you haven't done Walk #4 and time permits, you may follow the snaking, descending trail all the way down to the chairlift base station. Or, you can return to your car by taking the chairlift down.

Walk #8: Passo San Pellegrino/Albergo Miralago to Rifugio Fociade to Miralago

Walking Easy Time
3 hours

The walk to Rifugio Fociade (#607 on the map) begins at the high point on the Passo San Pellegrino at 6296 ft. (1919 m.), reached by driving to Moena and into the Valle di Pellegrino towards Falcade. The Albergo Miralago is just off the main auto road that goes through the pass, and the walk starts at the little lake next to the hotel.

The unused jeep road rises gently from 6299 ft. (1920 m.) to the Rif. Fociade at 6503 ft. (1982 m.), passing through the tiny hamlets of Gherghele and Sprinz, in the shadow of the high mountains of the Costa Bella, Sasso Valfredda and Sasso Vernale groups. The walk back is along the same track, with new views of the Dolomites across the Pellegrino Valley. This walk will give *Easy Walkers* the opportunity of visiting the Pellegrino Valley southeast of Vigo.

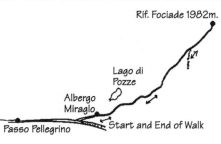

Rif. Fociade 1982m.

Lago di Pozze

Albergo Miraglo

Passo Pellegrino

Start and End of Walk

Walk #9: Walks through the Val di Fassa—Moena to Canazei

While the Val di Fassa is usually bathed in bright sunshine, you might wish to take a low-level walk due to inclement weather or just "tired legs." There are *passeggiate* along the valley, never very far from the auto road, many on easy, paved paths, some of which rise gently through the low foothills on either side of the valley. You should follow the Val di Fassa local maps—Vigo, Moena and Canazei—available free of charge at the Tourist Offices.

Above: First Snow on the Tofane

Below: Rosengaren Trail near Vigo de Fassa

Above: The Wall of Mt. Civetta overlooking Alleghe

Below: Trail from Dantercepies to Corvara

C. Lipton

Above: Tranquil Lake Alleghe

Below: Tre Cimi, near Cortina

Stefano Zardini

C. Lipton

Above: Earth Pyramids of Segonzano

Below: Cinque Torri Trail near Cortina

C. Lipton

ALLEGHE

In the geological age of the Dolomites, Lago Alleghe is "the new kid on the block," formed only 200 years ago when a giant landslide destroyed a dozen tiny villages and hamlets and formed this serene lake. The lakeside village of Alleghe, at 3212 ft. (979 m.), is off the beaten path in the Agordine Valley. The surrounding breathtaking scenery includes close-up views of the impressive wall of Mt. Civetta, 10,564 ft. (3220 m.), towering above lake and village, one of the most compelling images in the Dolomites.

Alleghe offers *Easy Walkers* a different type of alpine walking holiday. During early mornings and late afternoons this peaceful, trout-filled lake reflects rugged peaks and dark pine forests, in dramatic contrast to the high-altitude scenes of the sharply shadowed crevasses of the "pale Dolomites." After-dinner walks along the lake add a pleasant dimension not available in most other alpine base villages.

Invigorating hikes and excursions are available through-out the Agordine Valley. Malga Ciapela, at 4447 ft. (1446 m.), a few dozen kilometers from Alleghe, is the site of a triple cable car lift, and a not-to-be-missed, sensational visit to the Marmolada glacier at 10,965 ft. (3342 m.), a popular destination for summer skiers. Still visible on the glacier are signs of the bitter fighting that took place between the moun-tain troops of Italy and Austria during the first world war.

The relatively new Fedaia mountain pass drive to Lago di Fedaia at 6896 ft. (2100 m.) is on the border between the provinces of Belluno and Trentino, where *Easy Walkers* can take a level walk along the reservoir and ride in an unusual, two-person, open-bucket, standing lift to the lower side of the Marmolada glacier. A short detour to Rocca Pietore, while driving to Malga Ciapela and Lago di Fedaia, brings *Easy Walkers* to one of the prettiest villages of the Agordino and its notable parish church with an ancient, 16th-century triptych.

Agordo, south of Alleghe at 2005 ft. (611 m.), is the most important town in the valley. It is surrounded by forests and the famous Dolomite peaks of Agner, the Pale di San Lucano, Framont, the Moiazza, and the Cime di San Sebastiano. The town's central square is dominated by both the parish church, with its two towers, and the 17th-century Palazzo Crotta; this is a relaxing place to sit and enjoy a cappuccino and to watch the ever-changing views of the dramatic Dolomites.

The Agordo Valley stretches south for a *Walking Easy* visit to the old village of Canale d'Agordo, birthplace of Pope John Paul I. Canale sits at the head of an unspoiled valley, closed in between two groups of high mountains, with a popular walk through the Val Garés forest to the tiny, remote village of Garés. Of the six *Walking Easy* base villages in the Italian Alps, Alleghe is closest to Venice for a one-day excursion, only one and one-half hour's drive past Belluno.

While Lago Alleghe is serene, many of the area hikes are challenging, with ascents to the mountain *rifugios* of Coldai and Venezia—the unspoiled realms of eagles, marmots and chamois even higher up in the mountains. Other hikes take *Easy Walkers* to picturesque valleys, rushing waterfalls, through cool forests—with a comforting blaze on a rock or tree and directional signs always nearby. Not many Americans or British have discovered this treasure of a village and its tiny lake, surrounded by the stark beauty of the mountains and valleys of the Dolomites—a scenic and unique *Walking Easy* village.

Transportation to Alleghe

By Plane: The closest international airports to Alleghe are in Milan, Venice, and Munich, Germany. These cities have train or bus connections into Belluno, 30 miles (48 km) from Alleghe. Car rentals are available at all major airports.

By Train: The closest railroad station is in Belluno, with bus connections to Alleghe.

By Bus: You can take the Autolinea Gran Turismo bus to Alleghe at the Bologna Bus Terminal, or the local bus from Belluno.

Sample Bus Timetables:

Dep. Belluno	12:10 pm	
Arr. Agordo	12:48 pm	
Dep. Agordo	1:40 pm	
Arr. Alleghe	2:05 pm	
Dep. Milan	7:10 am	
Arr. Alleghe	2:05 pm	
Dep. Bologna	6:30 am	1:00 pm
Arr. Alleghe	11:35 am	6:15 pm

By Car: It is recommended that *Easy Walkers* **rent a car** if using Alleghe as a base village. Most of the hikes and sightseeing excursions require car transportation.

From north and west of Alleghe, exit *autostrada* A22 at Ora/Auer. Take highway 48 to Canazei over the Passo Pordoi. Near Cernadoi drive south to Alleghe. Or, exit A22 at Ora/Auer, take highway 48 to Moena and then drive east over Passo San Pellegrino to Alleghe. A third alternative is to exit A22 at Bressanone and drive by way of Corvara and Passo Falzarego to Alleghe.

From south of Alleghe use 203 from Belluno through Agordo to Alleghe.

From east of Alleghe at Pieve Cadore, take 51 and after a few miles, turn south on 347 at Venas to Forno di Zoldo and on to Alleghe.

Excursions in and around Alleghe

This section introduces day excursions for *Easy Walkers* to enjoy when the weather is not suitable for high-altitude walking or if an alternative to walking is desired. Be sure to check current timetables for best connections if using public transportation. The helpful Alleghe Tourist Office is in the center of town at Piazza Kennedy 17.

1. Lifts in and around Alleghe

A) Alleghe Funivie - Take this gondola for a 10-minute ride to Piani di Pezzè at 4823 ft. (1470m.).

B) Chairlift Piani di Pezzè - This lift picks up where the Alleghe Funivie leaves off, taking you on a 10-minute ride from Piani di Pezzè to Col dei Baldi. (See Walk #2 for more details.)

C) Marmolada Triple Lift - A visit to Marmolada, the highest mountain in the Dolomites at 10,968 ft. (3343 m.), on a *triple* cable car lift, is a must for *Easy Walkers*. After a short drive from Alleghe to Malga Ciapela, you will board the first of three cable cars taking passengers to the Marmolada glacier, largest in the Dolomites. While there are no walks here for *Easy Walkers*, this excursion should have a high priority on your "things to do" list.

2. Agordo - Agordo, population 4300, lies 12 miles (19 km) south of Alleghe and is the only sizeable town in the southeastern Dolomites. At 2005 ft. (611 m.), its elevation is fairly low compared to many other towns in Italy's Alps, but its location is superlative—it lies in an open hollow with a mild and reliable climate, surrounded by pine forests and majestic Dolomite mountain groups. A wide piazza sits in the center of town, dominated by a large, baroque church with a double bell tower. You might wish to visit the 17th-century **Palazzo Crotto.** Browse through the many shops on Agordo's streets or enjoy a cappuccino at one of the many outdoor cafés.

Directions: By car - Proceed south on 203 from Alleghe to Agordo. Reverse directions to return. By bus - The 9:33 bus from Alleghe arrives in Agordo at 10:10 am. To return, you can take the 4:10 bus arriving in Alleghe at 4:46 pm or the 5:00 bus, arriving in Alleghe at 5:36 pm.

3. Falcade - See the "Vigo di Fassa" chapter, Excursion #14.

Directions: By car - 203 south of Alleghe, turning right towards Canale d'Agordo and the Passo San Pellegrino. Reverse directions to return.

4. Colle Santa Lucia - Visit the historic church in this tiny village and note the view of Mt. Pelmo from the cemetery behind the church.

Directions: By car - North through Caprile, turning in the direction of Selva di Cadore. Reverse directions to return.

5. Selva di Cadore - At 4380 ft. (1335 m.) in the Val Fiorentina, on the south side of the Passo Giau, this village is in a sunny setting with dramatic views of Mt. Pelmo at 10,394 ft. (3168 m.). Selva di Cadore is a few miles northwest of Pescul and the chairlift used to reach the Fernazza Plateau, which is an ideal walking area.

Directions: By car - Drive north through Caprile, turning right at the sign to Selva. Reverse directions to return.

6. Cortina d'Ampezzo - See the chapter on "Cortina d'Ampezzo" for details.

Directions: By car - Head north out of Alleghe through Caprile, following signs to and driving over the Passo Falzarego to Cortina. Reverse directions to return.

7. Belluno - See the "Cortina d'Ampezzo" chapter, Excursion #14.

Directions: By car - Drive on 203 south through Agordo. When 203 splits, take the left or east fork into Belluno. Reverse directions to return.

8. Venice - See the chapter on "Venice" for details.

Directions: By car - Take 203 south through Agordo and when it splits, go east to 50 east and pick up *autostrada* A27 into Venice. You'll go over a long causeway and arrive at a busy and confusing area, the Piazza Roma, a dead-end for car traffic. On your right is a pair of large, eight-story garages where you can park your car. There can be a long line of cars trying to get into these garages if you don't arrive by 9:00 am. Walk from the garage across the top of Piazza Roma to the Grand Canal piers and take the large, inexpensive, public water-bus (Vaporetto) to San Marco. Reverse directions to return.

9. Padua/Padova - See the "Baselga di Pinè" chapter, Excursion #10.

Directions: By car - Follow 203 south through Agordo and, when it splits, take the left or east fork to Belluno and 50 east to the *autostrada* A27 south. At Mestre take the *autostrada* A4 west into Padua. Reverse directions to return.

10. Corvara - At 5145 ft. (1568 m.) and with a population of 700, Corvara lies below the towering Sasso Songher at 8743 ft. (2665 m.) and is the largest of the Tyrolean villages in the Val Badia/Gadertal region of the South Tyrol. This area is steeped in the Ladin culture and is quieter and less crowded than other South Tyrol resorts. Corvara is situated on a valley floor at the base of the Pralongia Plateau, with many shops and hotels close to the small, central piazza. The Col Alto lift rises from Corvara to the Pralongia Plateau and an excellent view of the surrounding mountains.

Directions: By car - 203 north to 48 west to Arabba where you pick up 243 north into Corvara. Reverse directions to return.

11. Canazei - Canazei lies on the main Dolomite Road to the famous Sella, Pordoi and Fedaia Passes. It is close to the Marmolada Range—known locally as the "Queen of the Dolomites"—and if you drive east of the village you'll have a superb view of this area, framed by the Catinaccio, the Towers of Vaioletto (Torri del Vaiolet), the Sella Massif and the Marmolada. Canazei can be an enjoyable village to explore on its own—with an interesting piazza, inviting shops, and the intriguing architecture of its old buildings.

Lifts in the Canazei area include **Pecol**, a cable car which lifts *Easy Walkers* to panoramic views of the Val di Fassa and the mountains surrounding Canazei, and the **Col dei Rossi**, a gondola adjunct of the Pecol cable car which rises even higher for spectacular views. Both lifts are open from 8:45 am to 12:30 pm and 2:00 to 6:00 pm.

Directions: By car - 203 north to 48 west, over the Passo Pordoi into Canazei. Reverse directions to return.

12. Pieve di Cadore - See the "Cortina d'Ampezzo" chapter, Excursion #3.

Directions: By car - North on 203 out of Alleghe through Caprile, to 48, turning east to 51 south into Pieve. Reverse directions to return.

Alleghe Walks

Recommended Maps

1) Carta delle Passeggiate - Dolomiti Agordine, available at the Tourist Office.

    A)Agordo, la Valle Agordina, Rivamonte Agordin.

    B)Cencenighe Agordino, Vallada Agordina, etc.

    C)Lago di Alleghe, Selva di Cadore, Colle S. Lucia

    D)Rocca Piétore, Arabba, Pieve di Livinallongo

2) Tabacco, #015 - Marmolada, Civetta

3) Tabacco, #025 - Dolomiti di Zoldo and Agordine

Walk #1: Introductory Walk around Lago di Alleghe

Walking Easy Time
1½ to 2 hours

This brief walk can be taken on your day of arrival and provides views of the lake, the pretty little gem of Alleghe, and the impressive Civetta wall, towering over the village.

Start: Leave from the Sporthotel Europa and walk to the right as you face the lake, going in a northerly direction with the lake on your left. Turn left at a path on the auto road and proceed until you arrive at a playground on the left. Walk through it to the canal and turn right, continuing on until you reach the bridge. Turning left, cross this little suspension bridge, then turn right on a narrow dirt path. Follow the earthen trail up and around to the left until you reach a small, paved auto road where you will turn left.

This short walk brings you to the other side of Lake Alleghe and a rarely used road which goes past the Disco Chalet de Lago, into the little village and the main road of Masarè. Walk along the path on the left side of the road, with the lake on your left, back to Alleghe. Note the gondola lift across the road on your right, which you will take on another day. Walk up the hill, past the ice rink, to the center of town, for a visit to the Tourist Office. A walk down the narrow, cobblestone street at the side of the church brings you back to the Sporthotel Europa.

Walk #2: Gondola and Chairlift to Col dei Baldi, Walk to Rifugio Coldai to Lago Coldai to Rifugio Coldai to Col dei Baldi

Walking Easy Time
3 to 4 hours

If you can tear yourself away from tranquil Lake Alleghe for a walk in the mountains, you will take the gondola from Alleghe to the mid-station at Pian di Pezzè at 4823 ft. (1470 m.) and transfer to the chairlift to Col dei Baldi at 6306 ft. (1922 m.). The walk proceeds gently downhill to 5844 ft. (1781 m.) and then rises up to Rifugio Coldai at 6995 ft. (2132 m.). For those with some energy left, the walk continues up to the ridge overlooking Lake Coldai at 7031 ft. (2143 m.). While this open, rocky trail ascends the mountain, it does so at a gradual rate, but it does steepen for the last 15 minutes before reaching the Rifugio Coldai. The views here are dominated by Mt. Pelmo rising to 10,399 ft. (3168 m.), across the valley, the site of two other *Walking Easy* excursions. As you reach the *rifugio*, the village of Pecol appears in the valley off to the right.

This is a popular hike, and you will share the trail with many other walkers, mostly Italian families out for an excursion. You will also notice serious hikers (denoted by the size of their backpacks), who will continue on this high, Dolomite trail, all the way to Rifugio Tissi at 7382 ft. (2250 m.) for a night's stay. Perhaps they will return to Alleghe the next day or continue on to another refuge along this famous Alta Via Dolomiti trail #1. The return to Alleghe is along the same trail, reversing your direction to the top station of the chairlift for the descent. There are restaurants and facilities at the lift stations and at the *refugio* and many opportunities for picnicking.

Directions: Turn left facing the lake from the front door of the Hotel Europa. Walking to the ice rink, turn left again once past the rink. Cross the auto road to the lift station Alleghe Funivie. Purchase a round-trip ticket to the top station and board the gondola for the ten-minute ride to Pian di Pezzè at 4823 ft. (1470 m.). Walk through the large parking lot, filled with cars of families who have come to this mid-station plateau for a day's outing. There are pony rides and restaurants and families spread on blankets picnicking and sunbathing throughout the meadow. Continue up to the chairlift station on the right for the next ten-minute ride to Col dei Baldi at 6306 ft. (1922 m.), where the walk begins.

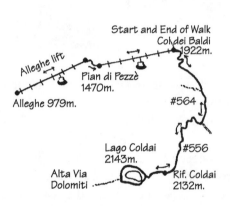

Start: After leaving the chairlift, walk straight ahead in the direction of Mt. Pelmo, the impressive mountain in front of you. Follow the red and white signs to Rif. Coldai, #561. Walk under the end of a ski lift on a wide path through a grassy meadow, which will probably be filled with cows. Bear right on the wide wagon path, instead of going over the mountain, and follow the trail down and around the meadow until you reach the restaurant in the valley below. It is possible to take some shortcuts down through the meadow directly to the restaurant, and that's okay, providing the trails are dry—if muddy they can be slippery. It takes about 30 minutes to reach this point. At the restaurant, bear to the right, following the sign for Rif. Coldai, #556. This is a rocky trail that immediately begins to ascend the mountain. There are many little shortcut trails, but we recommend that you stay on the well-defined main trail.

> ☞ **HINT:** *Easy Walkers* **should take this ascent at their own comfortable pace, allowing other hikers to pass, which they most certainly will! Rest as needed. The proper way to ascend is to take long strides, planting your heel firmly and leaning into the hill. The pace should be slow but steady. Be careful, this path is rocky—do your viewing standing still.**

The last few minutes of the trail is steeper, but manageable, if you rest as needed. The *rifugio* is a welcome sight and offers drinks, meals, snacks and facilities; it will be filled with hikers enjoying their holiday. If you wish, continue on the path up to the ridge for a view of the lake below, noting serious hikers continuing on for a night's stay at the Rif. Tissi along the mountain trail Alta Via Dolomiti. When ready, return by following the trail you came on all the way to the top station of the lift for the descent to Alleghe.

Walk #3: Walk and Excursion to Lago di Fedaia and Glacier at Marmolada

Allow the better part of a day for today's walk and excursion.

Today you will have an opportunity to go deep into the Dolomites for some fabulous views from 8859 ft. (2700 m.) at the foot of the giant glacier on Marmolada. You will also have the joy of driving on narrow, twisting Italian roads from 3281 ft. (1000 m.) at Alleghe through the Passo di Fedaia to the Fedaia reservoir at 6736 ft. (2053 m.). Restaurants and facilities are available at the *rifugios* and lift stations, but a picnic with views of Marmolada can be fun today.

Directions: Drive north in the direction of Caprile from Alleghe. At Caprile, turn left following signs to Rocca Pietore and Passo Fedaia. Drive through the tiny communities of

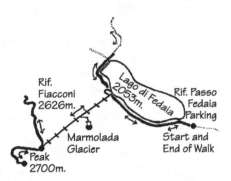

Bosco Verde and Malga Ciapela, the site of the start of a major triple lift to another vantage point of the glacier at Marmolada, an *Easy Walker* excursion for another day.

Start: Park your car at the Rifugio Passo Fedaia, a restaurant and souvenir store just before the reservoir, and walk ahead on an unused road along the left side of the reservoir. It is a 30-minute walk to the Marmolada bucket lift that will take you up to 8613 ft. (2626 m.) and the leading edge of the glacier. *Easy Walkers* have the option of joining many others for a rocky climb to 8859 ft. (2700 m.), about a 15-minute walk to the *rifugio* at the glacier. There is a steep, rocky trail descent which we do not recommend, but you will enjoy meandering through the rocky fields (or the snowy fields, depending on the month) as you look up at the glacier. Part of the thrill, other than the sensational views from Marmolada which reach to the jagged Dolomites around Cortina, is the open, standing, two-person lift cage that will take you up and down the mountain.

 HINT: It is suggested that you watch others get on the standing lift as it moves through the station. No more than two people are allowed, and the lift platform is

numbered where each passenger should stand just
before the open car arrives. There are attendants to
help you on and off, but you must be swift and hop on
as the car passes. The gate will be closed behind you.
Getting off at the top or bottom is also tricky—attendants will help—so move quicky.

When ready to leave Marmolada, board the lift car for
the breathtaking descent to the reservoir, observing hikers
climbing up and down the rocky trails below you. After getting off at the base station, walk across the top of the dam
to the other side and the trails that lead steeply up the mountain in front of you. Climb as far as you feel comfortable,
although strong hikers can reach the *rifugios* at the top.
Most of you will enjoy a grassy, meadow rest and/or picnic
with views of the lake, the glacier, and Marmolada.

Cross the dam and return to your car on the same traffic-free road at the side of the reservoir that you walked on
earlier. On the road back to Alleghe, you might enjoy stopping at the tiny, colorful village of Pian and visiting a few of
the interesting metal workshops.

Walk #4: Walk to Rifugio Citta di Fiume to Malga Prendera along Alta Via Dolomiti and Return

 Walking Easy Time
3 to 4 hours

This sensational hike will give *Easy Walkers* unparalleled
views of Mt. Pelmo and the impressive la Roccetta range,
on a pleasant ascending path through the forest and meadows. The day begins with an auto ride on a good mountain
road from Alleghe through Selva di Cadore to Pescul and
beyond. After parking, the trail rises gently from 5358 ft.

(1633 m.) to 6293 ft. (1918 m.) at the picturesque Rifugio Citta di Fiume. The path you will use today to the *rifugio* used to be an auto road. It is now closed to traffic and is well-used by hikers.

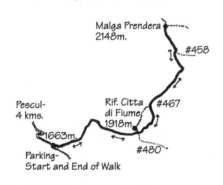

Malga Prendera
2148m.

#458

Pescul-
4 kms.

Rif. Citta
di Fiume;
1918m.

#467

1663m.

#480

Parking-
Start and End of Walk

After an hour's walk to the *rifugio*, the trail continues up to 6890 ft. (2100 m.) on an easily ascending, wide meadow trail for some spectacular views of the Agordino valley's jagged Dolomite peaks.

This second part of the hike, on the Alta Via Dolomiti Trail, will have walkers gasping at the beauty of la Roccetta. You will return to the *rifugio* and your car on the same path.

Directions: If you are in Italy you have to love to drive! However, it appears that the roads get a bit better each year, and we promise not to take you on any auto routes that are considered to be perilous. There may be a few moments when you hold your breath—just remember, let the passengers do the viewing while the driver concentrates on arriving at the destination safely.

To arrive at the start of today's walk, leave Alleghe to the north, driving through Caprile (**not** taking the cut-off mountain road to Selva di Cadore at the entrance to Caprile). Turn right at the second Selva sign and stay on the major auto road in the direction of Cortina, turning right at Rucava and following the sign to Selva di Cadore. Drive through Villagrande and Selva di Cadore, and about two and one-half miles (4 km) past the end of Pescul, after a major hairpin turn, you will see a large yellow and black sign and a parking area for the Rifugio Citta di Fiume on the left. The drive takes 30 to 35 minutes.

Start: The walk begins on the wide, unused road at 5456 ft. (1663 m.), blazed occasionally in red and white and marked #467. The road winds through the forest, with open views, and rises steadily but comfortably for an hour to the *rifugio* at 6293 ft. (1918 m.). You should stop here, on this lovely plateau; the popular *rifugio* provides picnic tables for visitors and a grassy meadow for sunning, along with spectacular views of Mt. Pelmo.

To continue, walk back down the road for a few meters, but turn left at the first intersecting path to a sign that directs you to the left on #467 (**not** taking #480 to the right). Follow the trail around and up the mountain. (It is possible to walk straight up the hill in back of the *rifugio*, as you may see others do, but it is easier to follow the directions above.) After ascending easily around the mountain to 6562 ft. (2000 m.), the path becomes fairly level, with outstanding views of the Dolomites on your left. As you walk and the sun changes position, the colors and shadows change also—a dramatic sight. After about 45 minutes, the path veers to the left at an open, grassy meadow, but walk onto the plain for magnificent views of la Rocchetta in front of you. It may be hard to tear yourself away—the photographic opportunities are endless!

When ready, continue back to the path, walking along the Alta Via Dolomiti trail, eventually leading to the Rifugio Croda da Lago Palmieri. The walk to the lake may be too long for *Easy Walkers* today—when you think it is appropriate, return on the same trail, leaving enough time to get back to your car. On your return drive you may want to stop and investigate some of the tiny, picturesque villages along the way.

 HINT: In Selva di Cadore, you'll see a sign taking you down to the left to Caprile. This is the little mountain road you did not take earlier. It is a shortcut and will

save you some time, but it starts off on a very narrow
road, and you might feel more comfortable returning
on the same road you came up on. After the first five
minutes, however, the road is excellent and it does cut
out ten to fifteen minutes of driving time.

Walk #5: Rifugio Staulanza to Rifugio Venezia to Rifugio Staulanza

Walking Easy Time
6½ hours

Mt. Pelmo is the center of attention on today's hike,
which extends halfway around the base of this imposing
mountain. After a drive from Alleghe to Passo Staulanza at
5794 ft. (1766 m.), you will hike along the Anello Zoldano
Trail from the western side of the mountain, around the
south, to the Rifugio Venezia at 6385 ft. (1946 m.) on the
east. If you have visited Citta di Fiume on another *Walking
Easy* hike, offering views of Pelmo from the north, you will
have viewed Pelmo from all directions.

This hike is a long one for *Easy Walkers*, and it will take
at least three and one-half hours to reach Rifugio Venezia.
With an hour's rest at the *rifugio* and a near three-hour walk
back, you will need a minimum of seven hours for today's
walk. This does not include the one-hour round-trip drive
from Alleghe or time spent for rest and photography. Still,
if you are out of your hotel before 9:00 am you should be
back by 5:00 pm.

The early part of the hike rises steadily on a forested,
mountain trail from 5794 ft. (1766 m.) to about 6234 ft.
(1900 m.). It then rolls on with little change in altitude until
you start to walk around to the east side of the mountain,

where there are some ascents and descents before reaching Rifugio Venezia at 6385 ft. (1946 m.). Experts who plan on climbing Pelmo often spend the night at this *rifugio* so they can get an early start in the morning for the challenging peak climb. Walkers are always on the trail for this popular hike which crosses all types of terrain—meadows, mountains, plateaus, and forests. Much of the early part of the walk is in the shaded forest, and it can be extremely muddy in spots, so this walk should not be taken after a rainy period.

This hike is rated more challenging, not because of its difficulty, but because of its length for *Easy Walkers*.

Directions: Leave Alleghe by car in the direction of Caprile, taking the second right turn on the major auto road to Selva di Cadore and watching for the sharp right to Selva di Cadore. Drive through Pescul for almost three and one-half miles (5.5 km), parking along the road in front of Rifugio Staulanza.

Start: The walk begins across the road from the *rifugio* on the marked route #472 to Rifugio Venezia. The path is signed and blazed all

the way, although just after beginning the walk up the hill, a branch of #472 splits to the left to Citta di Fiume. You will follow the markings to Rif. Venezia. Except for occasional variations, the path ascends on a narrow, rocky, dirt trail until you reach a plateau where the trail stays level for several kilometers. Your map shows this trail as #472 Anello Zoldano.

In about one hour there is a signed trail up to the left marked *dinosauri*, leading to the imprint made by a dinosaur millions of years ago, but you will continue on #472 to the *rifugio*. After leaving the forest, the views to the left are of the southern face of Pelmo, eventually changing to its rugged east wall. Views to the right are of ski trails across the valley and the little town of Zoppe in the valley below. At 6336 ft. (1931 m.) at a little intersection, cut sharply to the left, up to the *rifugio* at 6385 ft. (1946 m.), for a rest, scenery viewing, and lunch break. When ready, your trip back is along the same trail, and it will take about two and one-half to three hours to return.

Walk #6: Alleghe to Masarè to Sala to Forchiade to Masarè to Alleghe

Walking Easy Time
3½ to 4 hours

This low-level walk can be reserved for a cloudy day. *Easy Walkers* will proceed from Alleghe, along the road to Masarè, up the hillside overlooking the gorge and river. The altitude change is about 263 ft. (80 m.), gently ascending through le Foppe and bringing walkers down to Sala on a nice mountain trail through a cool pine forest. The return is on a path in the gorge, entered at the hamlet of Forchiade, and turning back to the road just before Masarè for the final walk into Alleghe. It is possible to extend this walk if you haven't already taken Walk #1 by continuing around the lake into Alleghe.

Start: Turn left as you leave the Sporthotel Europa. Walking along the lake, past the ice rink, turn right on the path along the auto road, with Lake Alleghe on your right.

Walk through Masarè and turn left into a parking area, just before the bridge over the river. Walk through the parking area to a paved road and turn right, and right again, on a wagon path. This logging road, lined with blueberry and raspberry bushes, rises gently from 3281 ft. (1000 m.) to 3491 ft. (1064 m.), bringing you to a sign directing you ahead to Sala. There are signed options that send stronger walkers up to Casamatta at 4147 ft. (1264 m.) and on to Rif. Tissi at 7382 ft. (2250 m.), not a recommended destination for *Easy Walkers* today.

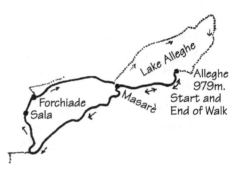

Pine needles cover this trail through the forest to Sala, as you descend several hundred meters into the old village. After passing some interesting old barns and houses, make a right turn onto the main auto road. Cross the bridge over the river and walk down to the right on the first paved road into the gorge in the direction of Masarè and Alleghe. At the split in the road, just past a few houses (Palle), stay to the left, not descending to the right down into the gorge.

This paved path eventually rejoins the main auto road, several hundred meters before Masarè, where *Easy Walkers* have the option of walking on the path next to the auto road and continuing on to Alleghe, or turning left on the road just before the lake and walking around the lake. If you choose this latter option, continue on the level, paved road, with the lake on your right, to the end of the road, where a sign directs you to Alleghe to the right down a narrow, dirt trail. This path leads you to the suspension bridge over the river, where you turn right again, back to Alleghe.

Walk #7: Excursion to Canale d'Agordo, Walk through the Val di Garès

Walking Easy Time
3 to 4 hours

Canale d'Agordo is an unspoiled treasure of a village, deep in the Agordo Valley. It is located off a road that traverses the mountains between the Agordine Valley and the Val di Fassa, at the entry point of the San Pelligrino Pass. Canale d'Agordo has managed to maintain its rich heritage, have restored barns and homes from past centuries (note the Casa delle Regole, in the center of town, dating from 1640). A walk through the tiny streets of the village will reveal the reverence that the local people feel for their community. The best way to discover Canale is to visit the Officio Turistico and speak with the enthusiastic director, Daniela Paolin, taking in as much information as you can and exploring all the nooks and crannies of this picturesque village.

Religion plays an important part in the lives of the townspeople. This is the birthplace of Pope John Paul I—the ancient church boasts a carved, wooden altar dedicated to him—and the village was also the recipient of a historic visit by Pope John Paul II.

Canale d'Agordo is also the start, after driving to a parking area on the outskirts of the village, of a walk through the Val di Garès. The walk begins on a wagon path through tall, pine forests at 3609 ft. (1100 m.). It proceeds along the picturesque Liera River and ascends gently through the Val di Garès to the tiny Lago di Garès at 4265 ft. (1300 m.), where walkers have several options. You can walk up and around the waterfall, coming down on a narrow, hillside trail into the tiny, remote hamlet of Garès at 4544 ft. (1385 m.), or turn right at the intersection just before the lake for a visit to Garès, with a return to your car on the same path you came on. It is possible to walk back to your car on the paved auto road on the other side of the river, but we think returning on the same path is cooler and prettier.

Directions: After packing a picnic lunch, drive south through Masarè to Cencenighe and make a right turn to Canale d'Agordo. Turn left into the village and park near the church. After a visit, continue driving through the village for a few kilometers until you reach a parking area on the left and the entrance to picnic grounds.

Start: Walk through the picnic grounds on the left, onto a pedestrian-only path, into the cool, shaded forest. This trail continues through the pine trees,

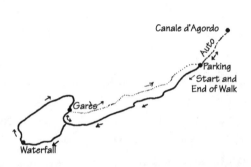

with the stream on your right, all the way through the Val di Garès, crossing the stream before reaching the little lake. *Easy Walkers* have the option of turning left, going around the lake and walking up to the waterfalls at Comelle, them continuing around and down a narrow hillside path to the tiny hamlet of Garès. Or you may turn right at the intersection before the lake and walk directly up to Garès. It is possible to walk back on a rarely used, paved road, or to return to your car by the same track you came on. It might be cooler and more scenic returning through the forest, however.

The following walks were not taken by the authors but were described to them by other Alleghe hikers.

Walk #8: Walk to Rifugio Falier with Optional Excursion by Triple Lift to Marmolada

Drive to Malga Ciapela, making a left turn past the campgrounds, along the Alta Via Dolomiti, and park at the end of the road. Walk up the trail—a short, steep climb—and go left on the unused auto road on #689. Turn right on mountain trail #610 that ascends along the Valle Ombretta, passing through Malga Ombretta at 6247 ft. (1904

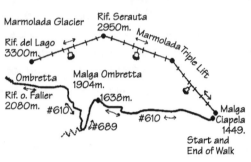

m.), and continue all the way to the Rifugio Falier at 6805 ft. (2074 m.). Return to your car on the same path. If time permits, drive back to Malga Ciapela and turn left to the Marmolada triple lift for a sensational cable car ride to the glacier at Marmolada at 10,663 ft. (3250 m.).

Walk #9: Passo Giau to Rifugio Averau and Return

Drive north from Alleghe through Caprile and Villagrande in the direction of Selva di Cadore, turning north at the major intersection and following the sign to Passo Giau. Park your car near the Rifugio Passo Giau at 7336 ft. (2236 m.) and walk north on the path past the *rifugio* to the fork in the road at 7363 ft. (2244 m.). Make sure you take the **left fork** signed #452, for a fairly level walk in the direction of Rifugio Averau. This path eventually intersects with an unused country road. Follow it up and around to the right, in the direction of Rif. Averau. The last part of this hike goes from 7487 ft. (2282 m.) to the *rifugio* at 7918 ft. (2413 m.). The views of the Nuvolau are reported to be spectacular. Return by the same route.

MERAN/MERANO

An alpine garden of eden, its streets and parks lined with palm trees, Merano lies in the heart of the Südtirol, in a wide, fertile and sunny valley with a delightfully mild climate, protected by the snow-capped peaks of the Italian Alps. In summer, nearby alpine pastures are covered with a carpet of colorful flowers and autumn brings an abundance of fruit in the many vineyards and apple orchards. Merano is a grand European resort, with elegant boutique shopping under 14th-century arcades, ancient churches and castles, notable museums and works of art, elegant, turn-of-the-century hotels, free daily concerts, a casino and racetrack.

An internationally famous health center, Merano's spas offer therapeutic treatments that rival the best in the world—the Spa Center on the banks of the Passer River is furnished with modern therapeutic equipment, including an indoor swimming pool filled with "thermal water." It is believed that freshly pressed grape juice, the "Meran Grape Cure," is beneficial for people with metabolic, heart and circulation problems, as well as kidney trouble and hepatitis.

There are hundreds of kilometers of walking paths in and around Merano's environs, bringing *Easy Walkers* to neighboring villages and tiny rural inns specializing in the best of local South Tyrolean cuisine. These trails will also lead you to the high mountains surrounding Merano, to grand castles and stark fortresses, and to the *waalwege*, gentle paths following the irrigation channels along the contours of hillside orchards and vineyards.

The Passer/Passirio River cascades through town under gilded, elegant bridges and is lined by gentle, tree-shaded walks—on one side the Winter Promenade and the other side the more shaded Summer Promenade. One of the most famous *Easy Walking* paths in Merano is the Tappeiner Way, named after the doctor who planned it, built it, and in 1892, donated it to the town. This path, with magnificent views over Merano and its valleys, meanders gently along the sides and slopes of Mt. St. Benedetto, from Merano to the Gilf ravine on the Passer River, and is bordered by tropical and sub-tropical trees and flowers.

Merano, one of the more sophisticated of the *Walking Easy* base villages recommended, makes great efforts to honor and keep its ancient traditions. There are weekly folklore evenings of singing and dancing in local Tirolese costume, the Grape Harvest Festival the second Sunday in October, and the Hafling horse race on Easter Monday.

The city first made its appearance in recorded history in the year 857, gradually assuming greater political importance, as witnessed by the large number of castles that can be visited. Its fame dates back to the 14th century when the castle of the Counts of Tirol gave the country its name and Merano was made the first capital. Its narrow, arcaded streets and ancient churches and castles still bear testimony to Merano's importance as the medieval capital of the Tirol. By the 15th century however, Innsbruck had become the capital, and Merano was no longer the home of princes—just a small country town surrounded by medieval walls.

This changed in the early 1800s when Merano first earned its reputation as a health resort, attracting members of European royal families, nobility and the aristocracy. It is currently a city of 34,000 residents—a holiday resort, a business center and a market town—the most popular destination in the Südtirol region of the Italian Alps. As mentioned previously, the Südtirol (or South Tyrol) was formerly part of Austria and was ceded to Italy over 75 years ago. Today the Südtirol is an autonomous province where all have the right to use and teach their native languages, a model for the treatment of linguistic and ethnic minorities in Europe.

The ancient city of Bolzano/Bozen is easily accessible to Merano and offers visitors a fascinating day excursion to the "old town" and to the Earth Pyramids on the Renon/Ritten Plateau above the city. Another day trip can take you south of Bolzano to the beautiful Kalterer See, where wine enthusiasts might enjoy visiting the Wine Museum in Ringberg Castle. One of the off-the-beaten-path valleys near Merano, the Ultental, with its high-alpine landscape and old farmhouses perched on steep mountainsides, is an unspoiled delight. The Passeiertal, with its spectacular waterfalls, has also retained much of its alpine individuality, and its high mountain passes lead into the Wipptal with the Timmelsjoch and the Jaufenpass, and the Ötztal of Austria. Many fascinating places, such as Innsbruck, Austria, and St. Moritz, Switzerland, are near enough to Merano to visit on a day trip.

Merano is a place to indulge yourself—to bask in the warmth of the sun, relax in the thermal baths, and enjoy the superb cuisine—while *Walking Easy* in the Italian Alps. Your itinerary should definitely include a week in Merano, one of the most beautiful towns in the Südtirol: charm, style, elegance and walking trails everywhere!

Transportation to Meran/Merano

By Plane: There are international airports in Milan and Munich, Germany, with train connections to Merano via Bolzano/Bozen.

By Rail: Train connections are available from Milan, Rome, Bologna, Venice, Innsbruck, Vienna, and Munich via Bolzano/Bozen, where trains run every hour for the 40-minute trip to Merano.

Sample Train Timetables:

dep. Munich	9:30 am	1:30 pm
arr. Bolzano	1:28 pm	5:45 pm
dep. Bolzano	2:00 pm	6:00 pm
arr. Merano	2:38 pm	6:30 pm
dep. Rome	7:30 am	1:50 pm
arr. Bolzano	2:17 pm	8:19 pm
dep. Bolzano	3:00 pm	9:00 pm
arr. Merano	3:38 pm	9:35 pm
dep. Milan	7:00 am	3:30 pm
arr. Bolzano	10:19 am	6:46 pm
dep. Bolzano	10:48 am	7:10 pm
arr. Merano	11:25 am	7:50 pm

By Car: From Bolzano, drive northwest on Route 38, following signs into Merano.

From Innsbruck, Austria, take the A13 *autostrada* (becoming A22 in Italy) south through the Brenner Pass, and exit at Bozen-Sud, picking up 38 to Merano. Or, shorter in mileage but perhaps longer in driving time because of the narrower roads, winding mountain passes, and scenerery stops, is A13 south from Innsbruck through the Brenner Pass, exiting at Vipiteno/Sterzing. Pick up 44 south, over the Jaufenpass, into Merano. The authors' favorite route from western Austria is 315 south from Landeck, crossing the Italian border at the gentle Reschenpass, the road becoming 40 in Italy, and continuing on 38 into Merano.

From St. Moritz and the Engadine area of Switzerland, take 27 north to Zernez, picking up 28 east to the Italian border at Mustair where the road becomes 41. Take 40 east and then 38 east into Merano.

From southern Italy, pick up A22 *autostrada* north, exiting at Bolzano-Sud and following 38 into Merano.

By Bus: Buses leave frequently from Bolzano for Merano—every 20 or 50 minutes depending on the time of day. The bus ride takes one hour.

The bus system in and around Merano is terrific. Use it wherever possible and buy a bus pass for economy and convenience. You can usually buy a bus pass at your hotel desk, tobacco shops, or the main bus station ticket office in Merano. A 25,000-lire pass entitles one person to unlimited bus rides during one week and must be shown to the bus driver.

A 10,000-lire pass entitles anyone using the pass to a set amount of bus trips. Each time you get on the bus you put the ticket into the machine and punch in the number listed to where you are going, i.e., Merano to Lana might be 09 on the ticket machine. The machine automatically deducts the correct amount of lire and shows you the amount left on the pass.

☞   **HINT: A complete bus schedule can be found in the booklet "A Guest in Merano," available at the front desk of your hotel.**

Activities in and around Meran/Merano

This section lists activities available in Merano on days when additions or alternatives to walking are desired. The helpful Merano Tourist Information Office is in the center of town at 45 Freiheitsstrasse, tel: 35223, next to the Kursaal.

Architecture - Stainach, Merano's oldest neighborhood, features narrow streets lined with ancient buildings. Three of the four original **city gates** are still standing: Bozen Gate on the south side of Merano, Passeirer Gate on the north side and Vinschger Gate on the west side. **Gunpowder Tower**, located on the Tappeiner Promenade, was mentioned in historical writings in 1377 and was used to store gunpowder after 1629.

Bowling - Ten-pin indoor bowling is at O.-Huber-Strasse, tel: 49461 to reserve lanes.

Casino - The Casino entrance is in the Kursaal on the River Promenade or from Freiheitstrasse. Opened in 1914, it includes the Pavillon des Fleur, built in 1874, with seating for 300, conference and reading rooms.

Castles - The 15th-century **Castle of the Counts (Landesfürstliche Castle)** is located behind City Hall on Galileistrasse and contains collections of furniture, weapons, paintings and tiled stoves. **Castle Tirol**, built between 1200 and 1300 near the town of Dorf Tyrol on the slopes of the Mutspitze, offers visitors a magnificent panorama of the Merano area. It has been restored and is now used in summer for concerts. Visit the archaeological museum and note the chapel portals. The first Tyrolean eagle, dating from about 1280, adorns the door to the Great Hall. Rebuilt in 1904, poet Ezra Pound's grandson now runs the agricultural museum housed at **Brunnenberg Castle**. **Rametz Castle**, built about 1200 and surrounded by gardens and vineyards, is now a wine-cellar near Rametz Bridge.

Churches - The **Parish Church of St. Nicholaus (Sankt Nikolaus)**, a 14th-century Gothic church with its ornate bell tower, stands in the heart of the "old town" on Piazza del Duomo and is a landmark of Merano. Inside the church are paintings and sculptures, and in the tower entrance are ancient frescoes. Behind the church are many old gravestones—until 1848 this was Merano's official cemetery. The gothic, octagonal **Church of St. Barbara (Cappella di Santa Barbara)** is located behind the cathedral and boasts a 15th-century Pietà. The **Chapel of St. Peter above Gratsch** features recently discovered and restored ancient stuccos and frescos from the 11th century.

Concerts - The town orchestra plays a concert every Sunday at 10:30 am at the open-air bandstand. Local bands in Tyrolean costume also appear at 5:00 and 10:00 pm under the central Merano shopping arcades, every second Friday of the month. Two open-air concerts are played daily from April to October by the Tourist Authority's resident orchestra at the open-air bandstand along the Passer Promenade, or in the Pavillon des Fleurs in inclement weather. The annual **International Meran Music Festival** is held in **Spa Hall**, considered to be the largest and most beautiful Art Nouveau building in the Italian Alps.

Fishing - The Passer and Etsch Rivers offer good fishing. Licenses are available at the Tourist Information Office.

Folklore Evenings - Enjoy singing and dancing with participants dressed in local Tyrolean costumes. Check with the Tourist Office.

Horse Racing - Located outside of Merano, one of the most beautiful tracks in the world is also the largest in the Alps. The Grand Premium Steeple-Chase is run the last Sunday in September in connection with a huge national lottery and brings together famous jockeys, horses and trainers from all around the racing world. The 5000-meter course features high fences and arduous water jumps—a challenge to horses and jockeys. Regular racing is held every Sunday evening.

Mini-Golf - Play in Marconi Park, near the Post Office, behind the Church of the Sacred Spirit on Innerhoferstrasse.

Monuments and Works of Art - Dating from 1919, the **Andreas Hofer Monument** is in the little park in front of the train station. Donated by the city of Milan and dedicated to the Alpine soldiers, the **Alpini Monument** is located in Mazziniplatz near the train station. A statue of Empress Elisabeth of Austria (the **Sissi Monument**) is on the Summer Promenade. The **Trogmann Monument** is located at the corner of Romstrasse and Blasius-Trogmann-Strasse. Note the **bust of Dr. Tappeiner**, creator of the Tappeiner Promenade. A 1706 **Statue of the Madonna** is on Sandplatz. There are busts of intellectual Beda Weber in Schiller Park, Prünster on the Tappeiner Promenade, and Redwitz, at the corner of Winkelweg and Parinstrasse. Pay a visit to the **Clarisse Convent,** inside and behind the Volksbank in Kornplatz, and note the old frescoes.

Museums - The **Civic Museum** is located on Galileistrasse—exhibits include four huge, carved, prehistoric stones found near Algund, Bronze Age artifacts, local arts and crafts, paintings and Gothic sculptures (hours: 10:00 am to noon and 4:00 pm to 6:00 pm, closed Saturday afternoon and holidays). The **Steiner Museum**, located near the cathedral, contains a collection of the artist Steiner's paintings, sculptures and wood carvings (hours: 11:00 am to 12:30 pm and 3:00 pm to 5:00 pm, closed Saturday afternoon and holidays).

Parks - Marconi Park is on Cavourstrasse, near the Post Office; its grounds are graced with many splendid roses. **Salvar Park** is at the Health Spa Centre and contains lovely palms. **Railway Station Park** has neat and colorful flower beds with a double line of fruit trees and crepe myrtle. **Mais Park** is on the corner of Winkelweg and Schafferstrasse, with box bushes, shrubs and other seasonal flora.

Riding - There is a riding school and stables at 2 E.-Toti-Strasse, tel: 32481 for information and rates.

Shopping - The **Meran Arcades**, Merano's main shopping street is lined with traditional buildings now housing modern shops and restaurants. Also, a large, bustling **weekly market**, primarily food and clothing, is held every Friday morning near the railroad station.

Skating - Available at the ice rink near the railroad station, 51 Meinhardstrasse.

Spas - On the banks of the Passer/Passirio River, the thermal spa center is furnished with the most modern equipment for treatment of illnesses and boasts an indoor swimming pool filled with thermal water, as well as doctors and technicians on hand to perform a vast selection of therapies. Merano is also famous for the autumn "grape cure" at harvest time. The freshly-pressed grape juice is supposedly helpful to those with metabolic problems, improving the heart and circulation systems, as well as helping patients with kidney and liver problems.

Special Events - These include the Easter Monday traditional race for Hafling horses and their "farmer riders" at the Merano Race Course, the Merano Gran Prix Horse Race and National Lottery on the last Sunday of September, canoe races on the Passer River in June and the Autumn Harvest Celebration on the second Sunday of October with bands, folklore groups and decorated floats.

Swimming - There is swimming at Public Lido, 20 Lidostrasse, with three heated outdoor pools, diving boards, games, large lawns, and a restaurant/café. Outdoor and indoor pools are at the Health Spa Centre on Thermanallee— a large park with an artifical lake and pools, restaurant and bar.

Tennis Courts - 11 courts are located on Piavestrasse, tel: 36550 for reservations and information.

Theatre - The **Meran City Theatre (Puccini Theatre)**, located in the center of town in Theatre Square, is an excellent example of the Liberty style of architecture and hosts performances by Italian and foreign theatrical companies.

Waterfall - Enjoy the waterfall in the Passer Ravine (Gilf) at the north end of the Summer Promenade and under St. Zeno Castle.

Excursions in and around Meran/Merano

This section introduces day excursions for *Easy Walkers* to enjoy when the weather is not suitable for high-altitude walking, or when an alternative to walking is desired. Be sure to check current timetables for best connections if using local transportation.

1. Lifts in and around Merano:

A) Chairlift from Merano (Galileistrasse) at 1050 ft. (320 m.) to Tirol Village and Segenbühel at 1673 ft. (510 m.), with a panorama of Merano and its surroundings. A restaurant and facilities are available.

B) Lift from Algund at 1312 ft. (400 m.) to Vellau at 2953 ft. (900 m.) with lovely walks, especially in spring and fall.

C) Lift from Vellau at 2953 ft. (900 m.) to Leiteralm at 4994 ft. (1522 m.) with a superb view of Merano and the surrounding valleys.

D) Lift from Vigiljoch to Larchbühel at 5971 ft. (1820 m.) and a fascinating panorama of the Dolomites.

E) Lift from Tall to Grube at 5932 ft. (1808 m.) and on to Sonntagsweide at 5315 ft. (1620 m.) on Hirzer mountain.

F) Lift from Falzeben at 5315 ft. (1620 m.) to Piffingerköpfl at 6232 ft. (1900 m.) and Kirchsteigeralm at 6396 ft. (1950 m.). From Kirchsteigeralm there are lifts to both Kesswandjoch at 7546 ft. (2300 m.) and Mittager at 7940 ft. (2420 m.).

2. Riffian - With a monumental **church** that is an important place of pilgrimage, the village of Riffian is east of Dorf Tyrol. The church houses a famous sculpture from 1420 and the adjacent **cemetery chapel** was constructed about 1400.

3. Schenna/Scena - On a hill across from Riffian, visit **Castle Schenna**, built in 1350, open now as a museum; the **Church of St. Martin**; and the neo-Gothic **Mausoleum** of the archdukes of Austria. Above Schenna is the small **Church of St. George**, a circular building built about 1200, with 15th-century Gothic frescos.

4. Bolzano/Bozen - See the "Selva/Wolkenstein" chapter, Excursion #3.

Directions: By car - Take 38 south, following the Bolzano/Bozen signs. Reverse directions to return. By bus - The 9:30 bus from Theaterplatz in Merano arrives in Bolzano at 10:32 am. To return, a 4:00 bus arrives in Merano at 5:00 pm. Buses run between Merano and Bolzano every 20 or 50 minutes, depending on the time of day. By train - The 9:40 train arrives in Bolzano at 10:20 am. To return, there is a 4:44 train, arriving in Merano at 5:27 pm. Trains run every hour to and from Merano and Bolzano.

5. Trento - See the "Baselga di Pinè" chapter, Excursion #8.

Directions: By car - 38 to Bolzano, following signs to the A22 *autostrada* south into Trento. Reverse directions to return.

6. Rovereto - See the "Vigo di Fassa" chapter, Excursion #7.

Directions: By car - Drive 38 south to Bolzano, taking the A22 *autostrada* south, exiting at Rovereto Nord and following signs into town. Reverse directions to return.

7. Egna/Neumarkt - See the "Vigo di Fassa" chapter, Excursion #8.

Directions: By car - Take 38 south to Bolzano, picking up the *autostrada* south and exiting at Ora - Egna. Follow the signs to Egna/Neumarkt. Reverse directions to return.

8. Vipiteno/Sterzing - 43 miles (69 km) north of Bolzano, Vipiteno is a picturesque town and a popular all-season resort. It is the first town of any size on the Italian side of the Brenner Pass from Austria. Walk down its main street, closed at one end by the **Torre delle Dodici**, erected in 1468, lined with 15th- and 16th-century Tyrolean houses, arcades and wrought-iron signs. Stop into the **Multscher Museum** in the Piazza Mitra to admire the 15th-century painted altar panels.

Because of its strategic location near the Brenner Pass, Vipiteno's stores offer an extraordinarily wide selection of merchandise: leather, wine and fashionable clothes from Italy; ham, sausage, bread and sports equipment from Austria and Germany. You can complete your trip by snacking on

Neapolitan pizza, Austrian strudel, or the local speciality *eisacktaler schlutzkrapfen*, a type of sweet doughnut.

Directions: By car - Take 44 north from Merano, through the Passeiertal, winding through the mountains over the Jaufenpass, into Vipiteno. Reverse directions to return.

9. Bressanone/Brixen - See the "Selva/Wolkenstein" chapter, Excursion #4.

Directions: By car - Drive on 38 out of Merano to Bolzano and take the A22 *autostrada* north to the Brixen-Pustertal exit, following local signs to Bressanone/Brixen. Reverse directions to return.

10. Chiusa/Klausen - South of Bressannone/Brixen, Chiusa has maintained its old Tyrolean character in its houses and wrought-iron signs. The **Parish Church** was finished in 1498 on the ruins of a 6th-century church, and the **Capuchin Monastery** was constructed in 1697. However, **St. Sebastian** is the oldest church in Chiusa, built about 1213. This round church can be found outside of town in an orchard. On a cliff 650 ft. (200 m) above the town, an ancient settlement known as the **Säben Cliff** was built, and in the 4th-century a church and fortifications were constructed. A **Benedictine Monastery** was built on the site in 1681, still standing today. The **Church of the Holy Cross** is part of the Säben Monastery, dating from the 17th century but standing on the original 8th-century church foundations on the high point of the cliff.

Directions: By car - Drive on 38 to Bolzano and pick up 12 north into Chiusa. Reverse directions to return.

11. Glorenza/Glurns - North of Merano in the Lower Vinschgau Valley (Val Venosta), not far from the Swiss border, Glorenza/Glurns has retained a great deal of medieval charm and contains high walls, three gate towers and four round corner towers. In fact, the town and its buildings are now protected by a preservation order and strict limitations are set on new building and remodelling. Ancient Glorenza was totally destroyed in 1499 after the German Emperor Maximilian lost a crucial battle to the Swiss. It was, however, rebuilt in the 16th century. Take special note of the old arcades where craftsmen now work, and enjoy the many pedestrians-only streets.

Directions: By car - Drive on 38 west out of Merano. At Schluderns, follow signs to Glorenza/Glurns. Reverse directions to return.

12. Verona - See the "Baselga di Pinè" chapter, Excursion #9.

Directions: By car - Take 38 to Bolzano, picking up the A22 *autostrada* south, then following local signs to Verona. Reverse directions to return. By train - The 6:25 train (with a change in Bolzano) arrives in Verona at 8:51 am and the 8:40 train to Bolzano (changing trains) arrives in Verona at 11:02 am. To return, trains leave Verona at 5:21 and 7:12, arriving in Merano (with a change in Bolzano) at 8:04 and 9:30 pm.

13. Ortisei/St. Ulrich - See Excursion #2 in the "Selva/Wolkenstein" chapter.

Directions: By car - Take 38 to Bolzano to 12 north to 242 east to Ortesei. Reverse directions to return.

14. Innsbruck, Austria - See the description in the "Selva/Wolkenstein" chapter, Excursion #10.

Directions: By car - 38 to Bolzano and the *autostrada* A22 north, through the Brenner Pass, becoming A13, into Innsbruck. Reverse directions to return. **Remember your passport!**

15. St. Moritz, Switzerland - The busy, year-round resort of St. Moritz is situated in a unique landscape of crystal-clear lakes, fragrant pine woods, imposing glaciers and majestic mountains, and boasts a long tradition as a spa town. The St. Moritz Tourist Office is located at via Maistra 12, in the main square past Hanselman's Tea Room, for additional information. Among the locale attractions are

Chesa Veglia, an old, Engadine house; the **Druiden Stone**, the site of the first settlers of the Engadine; the **Church of San Gian**, containing 11th- and 12th-century frescoes; and the Leaning Tower, the only remains of the original village built in 1193. Local museums include the **Segantini Museum**, with paintings by a well-known local artist, and the **Engadine Museum** and collections of rooms furnished in the local style with outstanding examples of *sgraffito*.

Directions: By car - Take 38 west (which becomes 40), to 41 west (which becomes 28 as you cross the border into Switzerland). At Zernez pick up 27 south into St. Moritz. Reverse directions to return. **Remember your passport!**

16. Bus tours - If you prefer public transportation on excursions around Merano, contact the Tourist Bureau. There are bus trips to: **Venice, Lake Garda, Val Gardena/Alpe di Siusi, St. Moritz, Verona, Ritten/Renon** outside of Bolzano to the **Earth Pyramids, Kaltersee/Lago di Caldero** and **local vineyards**.

Merano Walks

Recommended Map:
Kompass Wanderkart Carta Turistica #053 - Meran/Merano, 1:25,000, 1994/95

A little bit about *Waalwege* walks - When the snow melts in the mountains around Merano, the water is caught in a system of irrigation channels called *waale* in German. This water is used to irrigate the apple orchards and grape vineyards planted on the terraced hillsides and in the valleys. The path alongside the *waal*, known as a *waalweg*, is usually reached by an ascent on the road, but is level once it has been attained. Although this system of irrigation has been replaced in many places by mechanical irrigation, most of the *waale* are kept working, and the paths are well-groomed, well-signed, and very popular (with *winestubes* and restaurants located on the paths). An interesting note about the *waale*: the man taking care of a *waal* (a *waaler*) listens for the water bell (*waalschelle*). If the noise has stopped he knows that something is obstructing the water, which makes the device turn and the bell ring, and he investigates.

Walk #1: Algund along the Algunder Waalweg and Tappeiner Weg to Merano

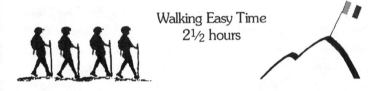

Walking Easy Time
2½ hours

This gentle walk is a good introduction to the marvelous walking around Merano, with views not only of this medieval town, but also of the thousands of acres of grape vineyards and apple orchards that fill the fertile valley. The walk can also be taken on an overcast day as an alternative to high mountain hiking. The first part of the walk, on the Algunder Waalweg, is reached by a short bus ride from Merano to the little village of Algund. After an hour the *waalweg* ends and you will descend to Merano on the famous Tappeiner Weg, and walk through the ancient shopping arcades back to your hotel.

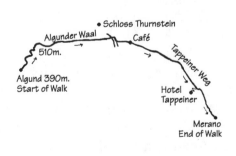

Directions: Take the #13 bus, getting off at Algund village center (the post office).

Start: Walk back down in the direction the bus came from, and after passing a little bakery on the left, turn left up the hill in the direction of the small Waalweg sign. Follow the quiet, winding, paved road, ascending steeply in the direction of the Waalweg. Cross the first auto road, continuing up, and in about 30 minutes you will reach a group of signs, one of which directs you to the right to the Algunder Waalweg. Once on the path alongside this miniature irrigation canal, you will be walking through grape arbors and apple orchards with views of the Meran valley down on your right.

After another 30 minutes, with imposing Schloss Thurnstein high on your left, the *waalweg* ends at another paved auto road. Turn right and in a few minutes you will come to the entrance of the famous Tappeiner Weg, for a leisurely one-hour stroll into Merano. Just after entering the Tappeiner Weg, you might wish to stop at Café Unterweger for a lunch and/or snack, enjoying its local cuisine and superb views of Merano.

Walk #2: Ifinger Lift to Piffing, Merano 2000, Walk to Meraner Hütte to Falzeben to Hafling

 Walking Easy Time
3½ hours

One of Merano's frequent buses will take you to the base station of the Ifinger Lift where you will board the cable car to Meran 2000 and the Chalet Piffing at 6250 ft. (1905 m.). The first part of the hike takes you down through the forest on a mountain trail. Eventually you will proceed up to the Meraner Hütte at 6431 ft. (1960 m.), after passing Kirchsteiger Alm. There are several ski lifts in the area, operating only in winter, as well as starting points for hikes to higher altitude destinations that *Easy Walkers* may choose to take on another day.

A treat is in store for you today, as the regional specialties at the Meraner Hütte are worth stopping for. There are several chefs behind a cafeteria-style counter serving traditional Südtirolean cooking such as kaiserschmarren, knödelsuppe and bratwurst. After indulging a little, the walk continues from the Meraner Hütte down to Hafling, through

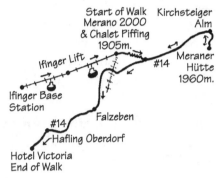

Falzeben, for the bus back to Merano. It's a good idea to have a bus schedule with you (available at the tourist office).

Directions: Take the bus (across from the Hotel Minerva) for the ride through Maia Alta to the Ifinger Lift Station, and purchase a one-way ticket to the top station at 6250 ft. (1905 m.).

Start: Follow the sign at the Piffing Restaurant to Meraner Hütte, walking straight ahead on the wide road. You will shortly turn off to the right on a narrow mountain trail marked "Meraner Hütte" that descends through the forest. After about 20 minutes the path spills out onto wagon trail #14. You will ascend gently from 5971 ft. (1820 m.) all the way up and around, passing Kirchsteiger Alm and its restaurant, as you turn right up the wagon path to the Meraner Hütte at 6431 ft. (1960 m.).

After resting and perhaps tasting the regional cooking at the restaurant, return by the same trail until you reach the little path coming out of the forest that you walked on earlier today. Stay to the left on the road for a gentle descent, following signs to Falzeben on #14. You will be viewing the top Piffing cable station up on the mountain to your right. It is possible to return by bus to Merano from Falzeben, but if the weather is nice, you might continue walking down to Hafling, where there are numerous opportunities to return to Merano by bus. The #14 path from Falzeben leaves from a small chalet at 5512 ft. (1680 m.), just to the right of the road, and descends to 5414 ft. (1650 m.). It crosses the road several times as it continues to descend towards Hafling/Oberdorf, and eventually you will come to a sign for the Hotel Victoria, across from the bus stop, for the return to Merano.

Walk #3: Dorf Tirol Lift to Hochmut, Walk to Tiroler Kreuz to Schloss Tirol and/or Schloss Brunnenberg to Dorf Tirol

Walking Easy Time
3 to 4 hours

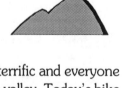

The bus system in Merano is really terrific and everyone uses it to reach locations throughout the valley. Today's hike leaves from Dorf Tirol, a short bus ride from Merano. A second bus takes you from Dorf Tirol to the base station of the Dorf Tirol-Hochmut Lift at 2133 ft. (650 m.).

The walk begins at Hochmut, 4465 ft. (1361 m.), and descends through Talbauer, 3967 ft. (1209 m.). The path heads down through the forest on the Muter Weg, with occasional scenic views of Dorf Tirol and the Passeiertal, all the way to Tiroler Kreuz at 2645 ft. (806 m.). You will return to Dorf Tirol along the road and visit one or both castles—Schloss Tirol and Schloss Brunnenberg—before returning to Dorf Tirol for the bus back to Merano. For those who would like to extend today's hike, it is possible to descend from

Schloss Brunnenberg on a trail down to Café Unterweger and return to Merano along the Tappeinerweg.

Directions: Walk down the street from the Hotel Minerva, turning right at the corner and walking one block to the bus stop for Dorf Tirol, a 10-minute bus ride. Please note that the schedule for Dorf Tirol is on the back of the schedule sign. At Dorf Tirol, take a second bus for the quick ride to the Hochmut Lift and purchase a one-way ticket to the top.

Start: After reviewing the signs at the Hochmut top station, walk to your right, departing from the front of the little restaurant and following the signs to Dorf Tirol. This mountain trail is largely in the open as you wind around the valley, with views of Dorf Tirol below on the right. The trail descends on #24 to 3967 ft. (1209 m.) at the Talbauer Restaurant, and in another few minutes, it descends further to your right at a fork in the trail. The left path (#24 Meraner Höhenweg), ascends towards Longfallhof, another *Walking Easy* hike. The path to the right descends through the forest and is signed towards Dorf Tirol, #23 Muter Weg on your map, by way of Tiroler Kreuz at 2645 ft. (806 m.). There is a cut-off toward the bottom of this trail marked "Farmerkreuz." Do **not** take that trail but continue on the main forest path to Tiroler Kreuz.

The path eventually comes out onto a road in front of the Tiroler Kreuz Restaurant, and it is possible to take a bus back to Dorf Tirol from here (running every 20 minutes). But it is a short, pleasant walk to Dorf Tirol, where you can visit one or both of the castles— Tirol and Brunnenberg. The closest castle is Schloss Brunnenberg, on a road just outside of Dorf Tirol, easily acces-

sible from the middle of the village. It is possible to walk down from the back of the castle to the Tappeinerweg, for a pleasant hour's walk to Merano, or you can reverse your direction back to Dorf Tirol for the bus to Merano.

Walk #4: Forst to Lana along the Marlinger Waalweg

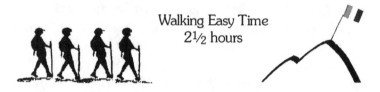

Walking Easy Time
2½ hours

Today's popular, low-level walk takes place on the Marlinger Waalweg, passing through the apple orchards and grape arbors on the gentle slopes along the Merano valley. You will take a bus from Merano center for the short ride to Forst, with its famous brewery, where the walk begins. It is necessary to ascend along a road for about 20 minutes before accessing the *waalweg* path. The Marlinger Waalweg runs north-south, as if on a low balcony overlooking all of Merano, with views from the Passeiertal, along the Passer River, past Lana to the south. There is a higher balcony walk above the *waalweg*, the Marlinger Höhenweg that *Easy Walkers* can take on another day. The entire length of the walk traverses orchards and vineyards famous for the

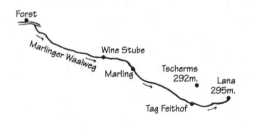

special Meran grapes, and along the way, and *winestubes* and restaurants are strategically located for rest and relaxation. The path ends above Lana, where you will take the bus back to Merano.

Directions: Take bus #11 at Theaterplatz/Piazza Teatro, for the short ride to Forst. Get off the bus at the last stop in Forst.

Start: Cross the road and walk up the gently ascending auto road, following the sign to the *waalweg*. Once there, walk in the direction of Merano, following the *waalweg* signs, past Marling, perhaps stopping at the little *winestube* for *traubensaft* (freshly harvested grape juice) and thick pretzels. The *waalweg* ends in the hills above Lana. Follow the signs into town and the bus station and take the Lana bus to Merano.

Walk #5: Dorf Tirol Lift to Hochmut, Walk to Longfallhof on Meraner Höhenweg to Tiroler Kreuz to Dorf Tirol

Walking Easy Time
4 hours

This hike starts from Hochmut at 4466 ft. (1361 m.), after taking the bus to Dorf Tirol from Merano. The beginning of the hike is similar to Walk #3, but after descending to Talbauer at 3967 ft. (1209 m.), you will shortly take the left fork on Meraner Höhenweg #24, instead of descending directly to Tiroler Kreuz. The Meraner Höhenweg climbs on a more challenging, but well-defined, mountain trail, through the forest, up to 4758 ft. (1450 m.). It descends again, at times somewhat steeply, to the road below Longfallhof at 3527 ft. (1075 m.), for the walk back to Dorf Tirol through Tiroler Kreuz. This walk can be shortened by taking the bus, running every 20 minutes, from Tiroler Kreuz to Dorf Tirol.

Directions: Walk down from the Hotel Minerva and make a right at the corner. The bus stop to Dorf Tirol is on the next block, with buses running to and from Dorf Tirol every half-hour. Get off at Dorf Tirol and change for the short ride to the Dorf Tirol-Hochmut lift station. Purchase a one-way ticket to the top.

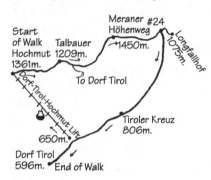

Start: Follow mountain path #24, in front of the restaurant, in the direction of Talbauer and Dorf Tirol. The trail descends around the mountain to 3967 ft. (1209 m.) at the Talbauer Restaurant and soon forks up the mountain to the left—do **not** take the right path down to Dorf Tirol. The trail climbs through the forest, ascending about 820 ft. (250 m.)—be careful, it can be slippery—before descending to the auto road just before the Restaurant Longfallhof. Make a right turn on the road for the easy walk to Tiroler Kreuz at 2645 ft. (806 m.). You have two options here. You can wait for a bus that comes every 20 minutes for the short ride into Dorf Tirol and the bus back to Merano, or continue walking on the road into Dorf Tirol for the bus to Merano.

Walks #6 and #7 were suggested by guests at the Hotel Minerva.

Walk #6: Dorf Tirol Lift to Hochmut, Walk on the Hans-Friedenweg to Leiter-Alm to Vellau, Bus Return to Merano

Walking Easy Time
4 to 5 hours

This walk has some rocky ascents and steep descents but should present no problems for experienced walkers. Taking the Dorf Tirol Lift to Hochmut at 4466 ft. (1361 m.), you will walk on the Hans-Friedenweg to Leiter Alm at 4994 ft. (1522 m.). From here you may either walk or take the gondola down to Vellau at 3170 ft., where you will pick up your bus for the return to Merano.

Walk #7: Merano to Schenna to Merano

Walking Easy Time
3½ to 4 hours

Walk along the Passer River on #5 on your map, making a right turn across the bridge, just past Schenna, high up on the mountain. Walk up to Schenna for a visit to this lovely, hilltop town and its castle, Schloss Schenna. Return to Merano by bus or by walking along the Passer River on the Schenna side on path #4.

There are several short, gentle, promenade walks in and around this beautiful town.

Promenade Walk #8: Gilf (Ravine) Promenade

Walk from the Roman Bridge built in 1620 into the Passer ravine, with its rich vegetation, up to the Tappeiner Way.

Promenade Walk #9: Passer River Walk

Walk on the right bank of the river from the Post Office Bridge to the Railway Bridge, passing the open-air bandstand and many delightful flowers and shrubs.

Promenade Walk #10: Winter Promenade

This path is on the right bank of the Passer River from the Post Office Bridge to the Roman Bridge, with sheltered, covered arcades of climbing plants and two beautiful tulip trees flowering right in the middle of the Promenade.

Promenade Walk #11: Summer Promenade

On the left bank of the Passer River, opposite the Winter Walk, the delightful statue of Empress Elisabeth of Austria stands among the trees on this path—this is a shady walk for a hot day.

BASELGA DI PINÈ

The province of Trentino, in the northern portion of the Italian peninsula, extends from the Val di Fassa and Canazei in the north, to the tip of Lake Garda in the south. The ancient city of Trento is at the heart of the province and serves as the pulsating hub of its commercial and cultural activity.

Baselga di Pinè, near Trento in the center of the Trentino, was chosen as an *Easy Walker* base village because it offers a different type of alpine walking experience. The wide, green, tranquil Pinè Valley is dotted with meadows, lakes, vineyards, orchards and farms, and the gently rolling rural landscape is in sharp contrast to the starker images of the northern Italian Dolomites. After centuries of agricultural endeavor, the Pinè Valley still supports a traditional forest-pastoral economy, with quarrying, timber, and berry farms—strawberries, raspberries, blackberries, blueberries and currants—the main industries.

In the neighboring Cembra Valley, vineyards are everywhere. Rising vertically from the valley floor to bright blue, cloudless, summer skies, row upon row of apple orchards and heavily-laden grape arbors crowd the mountainside with a mathematical precision that first pleases, then baffles the eye. Here, crates line the fields, ready to receive the fruit, while families burdened by old woven baskets, stained with sweat and juice, noiselessly harvest the plump, robust grapes. This slow, sometimes painful, but always joyful dance is performed only once a year in celebration of autumn's bounty.

Baselga di Pinè is also situated close to two beautiful lakes—Lago di Serraia and Lago di Piazze—both encircled by walking trails, with opportunities for sailing, swimming and fishing. Winter sports are popular in this area, with hundreds of kilometers devoted to cross-country skiing and ice surfaces for speed and figure skating. Baselga is home to one of the most important ice skating rinks in northern Italy, made famous by Roberto Sighel, the 1992 world speed skating champion, who lives and trains in a suburb of Baselga. This rink will proudly host the 1995 Men's World Championship speed skating races.

There are opportunities for varied excursions from the simple village of Baselga. One excursion will take *Easy Walkers* to Piazzo in the nearby Cembra Valley, with a visit to the ruins of Castel di Segonzano and a visually stimulating walk through the vineyards and apple orchards. The geologically mystifying Earth Pyramids of Segonzano, also in the neighboring Valle di Cembra, shouldn't be missed; while the medieval cities of Verona, Padua and Venice can provide a breathtaking contrast from natural to man-made wonders.

The Altopiano di Pinè or the plateau of Pinè, 2625 to 3280 ft. (800 to 1000 m.), at the foot of the Lagorai mountains, is distinguished by its forests, its glacial lakes, its nature reserves and its berry farms. It, too, is criss-crossed by walking paths through a part of the Italian Alps still unspoiled and undiscovered by most Americans and Europeans.

Transportation to Baselga di Pinè

By Plane: There is an international airport in Milan, 149 miles (240 km) from Baselga. A change of plane is necessary to fly into airports in Verona, 68 miles (110 km) away, and Venice, 93 miles (150 km) south. Verona is a one and one-half hour drive from Baselga. Venice is two hours, and Milan is two and one-half hours.

By Train: The nearest train station to Baselga is in Trento, where there is bus service to Baselga di Pinè.

By Bus: Buses leave to and from Trento, 11 miles (18 km) away, about six times a day.

Sample Bus Timetable:

Dep. Trento	8:30 am	12:10 pm
Arr. Baselga	9:22 am	1:02 pm

By Car: *Note!* If you are planning a Walking Easy holiday in Baselga di Pinè, a car is a necessity for excursions and for arriving at the start of walks.

If you fly into Venice and rent a car, take *autostrada* A4 west and pick up route 47, turning off at Pergine on #66 and heading north to Baselga di Pinè.

Driving from the Verona area south of Baselga, or Bolzano from the north of Baselga, take A22 *autostrada* to Trento, picking up #47 east. After five miles (8 km), exit and take #83 to Baselga di Pinè.

Coming from the Fiemme and Fassa valleys, drive on #48 to #71 south through the Valle de Cembra and turn off at Sover, passing through Brusago and on to Baselga.

Activities in Baselga di Pinè

This section lists activities available in Baselga di Pinè on days when additions or alternatives to walking are desired. The very helpful Baselga Tourist Information Office, headed by Sergio Anesi, is at Via C. Battisti, 98, on the main street of the village, close to Lago di Serraia, tel: 461/557028.

Churches - This semi-rural area has many notable churches. The **Church of the Assumption of Mary (Santa Maria Assunta)** is on a small square surrounded by some of Baselga's oldest buildings (see Walk #2 for more details). At Miola, near the Ice Rink outside the main part of town, the **Parish Church of St. Rocco** was built in 1914 next to a 16th-century church sacristy. The wooden altar dating from 1694 was preserved in the new church, as were paintings and an altar piece from the 1600s. Note the elegant Renaissance portal of the old church, blending into the left chapel. The early 13th-century **Church of the Guardian Angels (Angeli Custodi)** is in Ricaldo, on the northern outskirts of Baselga; it contains an important silver Gothic chalice from the late 15th century, presented by Maximilian I to the church of St. Peter in Trento.

The **Church of Sternigo**, constructed during the 17th and 18th centuries and restored in 1940, features *graffito* frescoes. It is located at the edge of Baselga in the higher part of town, at the beginning of steep, terraced fields. Located southwest of the center of Baselga in the suburb of Tressilla, the **Chapel of St. Lucia** boasts a baroque altar of carved and decorated wood with an 18th-century dome. The **Church of St. Joseph** is south of Baselga in the hamlet of Vigo (see Walk #6 for more details). Montagnaga di Pinè's **Parish Church of S. Anna** is of note as a "Marian sanctuary" (see Walk #3 for more details). Also at Montagnaga, the **Comparsa** indicates the location where the Madonna appeared to Domenica Targa in 1729 and the **Monument to the Redeemer** commemorates the mystery of the Redemption (see Walk #3 for more details).

Festivals and Music Events - There are numerous musical groups, mountain choirs and bands in the Baselga area. Check with the Tourist Office for performances.

Fishing/Sailing - At 3183 ft. (970 m.), Lago di Serraia is at the foot of 6414 ft. (1955 m.) Monte Costalta. The lake was formed in glacial eras by the damming of the valley, and it is now a relaxing place to fish or rent a boat.

Mini-Golf - See the Ice Rink Pinè Olympic Artificial Ice Stadium or contact the Tourist Office for more details.

Mountain Biking - Rentals are available in Baselga. Contact the Tourist Office for further information.

Riding - The Ice Rink Pinè Olympic Artificial Ice Stadium has a fine equestrian center.

Skating - The Ice Rink Pinè Olympic Artificial Ice Stadium will host the World Speed Skating Championships for men in 1995. The speed skating rink is outdoors, but there is also a hockey rink which is enclosed separately.

Tennis - There are several courts at Ice Rink Pinè Olympic Artificial Ice Stadium.

Windsurfing - There is a windsurfing school at the Ice Rink Pinè Olympic Artificial Ice Stadium.

Excursions in and around Baselga di Pinè

This section introduces excursions for *Easy Walkers* to enjoy when the weather is not suitable for high-altitude walking or when an alternative to walking is desired. Be sure to check current timetables if using public transportation.

1. Earth Pyramids of Segonzano (Le Piramidi di Terra di Segonzano) - Erosion has formed these Cembra Valley cone-shaped trunks, surmounted by rocks, many weighing over 22,000 pounds. Some have likened the effect to that of pipe organs topped by boulders, towering over the surrounding vegetation. (See Walk #4 for more details.)

Directions: By car - Drive south in the direction of Trento. After a little more than two miles (3.5 km), take the right turnoff signed "Segonzano" and turn right again when reaching the main auto road. Drive to the large parking area at the pyramids. Reverse directions to return.

2. Nature Reserve of Laghestel - In the thick pine woods outside Baselga lies a strip of protected bush interspersed between peat bog swamps, which comprise a natural refuge and habitat for many species of flora and fauna. (See Walk #6 for more details.)

3. San Mauro di Pinè - The **Church of San Mauro** was in existence in the early 13th century. Note the facade with its Renaissance atrium. The Gothic interior boasts a triptych of carved, gilded and painted wood.

Directions: By car - Drive south in the direction of Trento. Note the sign to S. Mauro and turn right. The road ends at S. Mauro. Park and walk up to the church. Reverse directions to return.

4. Bedollo - Visit the **Church of S. Osvaldo**, its high, stone walls rising majestically above a terraced crag, next to the onion-domed, spire bell-tower built in 1775.

Directions: By car - Drive north from Baselga a few miles to Bedollo. Reverse directions to return.

5. Fornace - The **Castle at Fornace** has no written documentation of when it was built, but a history of the Lords of Fornace notes its existence in the year 845. In the mid-1800s the castle was demolished to build a church, but in the 1970s the province of Trento carried out extensive restoration of the remaining castle structure. Medieval and renaissance ceramics recovered in the restoration of the Roccabruna Castle of Fornace are now displayed in an area called "At the table with the lords of Fornas" ("A tavola con i signori di Fornas").

Directions: By car - Drive south out of town, turn sharply right and down hill at the sign to Segonzano. At the main road follow the sign up to Fornace. Reverse directions to return.

6. Civezzano - The **Parish Church of the Assumption** is of interest because of the Renaissance architecture of its pilasters, capitals and portals, although it is Gothic in plan, vault, windows and arches. It is among the oldest and best-known churches in the Trentino area.

Directions: By car - Drive south out of town, turning right on #47 and right again to Civezzano. Reverse directions to return.

7. Riva del Garda - Situated on the northern tip of Lake Garda, this town's excellent climate and strategic lake and mountain location make it one of Italy's premier resorts. The "old town" center on the lake front contains Venetian-Lombard architecture in its piazzas. Note the **Apponale Tower**, erected in the 13th century to defent the port, and the **Fort** itself, dating back to 1124, with four square towers and a drawbridge. Visit the 18th-century **Parish Church of the Assunta** and the **Church of the Inviolata**, with elegant, baroque construction.

Directions: By car - Drive south out of Baselga, following signs to Trento. Do not get on the *autostrada*, but take 45 west and south to Riva del Garda. Reverse directions to return, or to return via a circle route, taking 240 east to the *autostrada* A22, north to Trento, where you will pick up 47 east and then follow signs on the local road north to Baselga.

8. Trento - Stop by the Baselga Tourist Office and ask for the Orientation Map of Trento, to be used for this one-day tour. The capital of Trentino province has retained its architectural and artistic charm and is especially attractive in spring or during the fall harvest months. Trento is the local center for antiques, and a flea market is held in **Piazza d'Arogno** every third Sunday of the month, with a handicrafts market every Friday and Saturday. Parking is difficult in Trento and you might wish to use public transportation or park only in designated areas. In order to follow this itinerary, it is easiest to park at Piazza Fiera (#P5, on the map).

After exiting the parking area, walk to the right and make a right turn on via Mazzini, passing **Palazzo Larches-Fogarezzo** (#7) on the left. Continue on via S. Vigilio to the center of the city and visit the **Piazzo del Duomo** with the **Cathedral di S. Vigilio** (#39), at its southern end and the baroque **Fountain of Neptune** (#38), at the center of the square. Just across from the cathedral is the **Museo Diocesano Tridentino** (#M1) in the **Palazzo Pretoria**, built in the 13th century as the residence of the prince-bishops and now the home of the **Museo Diocesano Tridentino**, with artifacts from the cathedral's treasury.

Continue walking on via Belanzani, opposite the Neptune Fountain, past the **Palazzo Alberti-Colico** (#35), turning left to the Renaissance **Church of Santa Maria Maggiore** (#42). Return back up past the **Town Hall** on via Orne and turn left at **Teatro Sociale** (#23). Turn right all the way on via S. Marco to the moated **Castle of Good Council (Castello del Buonconsiglio)** (#2), its **Provincial Art Museum (Museo Provinciale D'Arte)** and the 13th-century **Eagle's Tower (Torre dell'Aquila)** (#M3). Walk back to your car by turning right on via Venezia, past **Palazzo Londron** (#8) to Piazza Fiera and the car park.

Directions: By car - Take the local road south out of town, following signs to Trento. Reverse directions to return. By bus - The 8:10 bus from Baselga arrives in Trento at 9:00 am. To return, there is a 2:35 bus arriving in Baselga at 3:00 pm and a 5:15 bus arriving at 5:57 pm.

9. Verona - This "Venetian Arc" city on the banks of the Adige River ranks second only to Venice as a tourist attraction in this part of Italy. Verona has a picturesque, medieval "old town" center, immortalized by Shakespeare in "Romeo and Juliet."

A good place to begin walking is at the **Piazza delle Erbe (Square of Herbs)**, with a colorful morning fruit and vegetable market; this is the location of the Tourist Information Office where you can pick up a city map and brochures. From here, walk to the **Piazza Brà**, a large and spacious square at the center of the city, and visit the **Arena di Verona**. Built by the Romans in the first century, this was among the largest arenas in the Roman world, accommodating 25,000 spectators—it has perfect acoustics and now hosts musical performances. The Arena is open Tuesday to Sunday from 8:00 am to 6:30 pm, with admission charge, except the first Sunday of each month when it is free.

Running off the Piazza delle Erbe is the **Piazza dei Seignori**, surrounded on all sides with stately old buildings, a **Statue of Dante** in its center. Check out the 12th-century **Palazzo della Ragione** and **Loggia del Consiglio**. At one end of the square is the **Palazzo del Governo** from where the Della Scalas once ruled Verona. Off this end of the square are the **Tombs of the Scaligers (Archa Scaligere)**, magnificent Gothic tombs of the ancient rulers of Verona. In the same area is the Gothic **Church of Sant'Anastasia** and the Romanesque **Cathedral (Duomo)**. Inside the Duomo, note the remarkable main doorway adorned with figures of the prophets, the classic red marble pillars, and the Titian altarpiece on the first altar to the left as you enter.

If you cross the Adige River at Ponte Nuovo, walk in the **Giusti Gardens (Giardino Giusti)**, the grounds of a palace dating from 1580, laid out in terraces and mazes. Walk up to the top on a shady path for a fine view of the surrounding countryside. The gardens are open daily from 8:00 am to 8:00 pm, with an admission charge.

If you recross the Adige River on Ponte Pietra, pick up Corso Sant'Anastasia which becomes Corso Porta Borsari and Corso Cavour, leading to the **Old Castle** and **Bridge of the Scaligers (Castelvecchio)**. This 14th-century castle, with massive walls, towers, turrets and a huge courtyard, contains a **Museum of Art** exhibiting paintings, sculptures, arms and jewelry. The Museum is open Tuesday to Sunday from 8:00 am to 6:30 pm, with admission charge. From the castle you can walk along Rigaste San Zeno and Via Barbarani to **St. Zeno Major (Chiesa di San Zeno Maggiore)**, one of the finest Romanesque churches in Northern Italy, set between two medieval bell towers.

Directions: By car - Take the local road south out of town following directions to Trento. At Trento, follow green *autostrada* signs (A22) south, then local signs into Verona. Reverse directions to return.

10. Padua/Padova - This busy, bustling city of over 240,000 inhabitants boasts a medieval "old town" with arcaded squares and dark, narrow, cobblestone streets. The Tourist Information Office can supply a city map and brochures for *Easy Walkers* to plan a walking tour of Padua's main sites.

Don't miss the **Scrovegni Chapel (Cappella degli Scrovegni)**, with its famous 14th-century frescoes by Giotta, open Tuesday to Sunday from 9:00 am to 7:00 pm, with an admission charge. Left of the Chapel entrance and across the gardens is the 13th-century **Church of the Hermits (Chiesa degli Eremitani),** containing fragments of frescoes done by Mantegna, many destroyed in 1944 in Allied bombings. The **Municipal Museum (Museo Civico)** is located in the **Monastery of St. Anthony** and is the home of many works by master Venetian painters.

On a side street leading off Corso del Popolo you'll find the 16th-century **University**. Note its perfectly proportioned anatomy theater and a hall with a lectern once used by Galileo. Admission is free but there are guided visits only. The **Saint's Basilica (Basilica del Santo)** overlooks a square with the 15th-century Donatello **Equestrian Statue of Gattamelata.** The Romanesque-Gothic style basilica was constructed from 1232 to 1307 with eight tiered domes.

The **Law Courts (Palazzo della Regional)** stand between the Piazza delle Frutta and Piazza delle Erba. Inside are 15th-century frescoes and a Donatello wooden horse. They are open from 9:00 am to 1:30 pm from Tuesday to Saturday, and 9:30 am to 12:30 pm on Sunday, with admission charge. **Piazza dei Signori** contains the **Palazzo del Capitanio**, where the Venetian governors resided from the 14th to the 16th centuries. The large 15th-century clock was the first of its kind in Italy. The **Botanical Garden**

(Giardino Botanico) is one of the oldest in Europe, laid out in 1545, and is open weekdays from 9:00 am to 1:00 pm, Sundays and holidays 10:00 am to 1:00 pm,with an admission charge.

Directions: By car - Take the local road south out of town, following signs to Trento. Pick up #47 and drive east and then south, through Bassano to Padua. Reverse directions to return.

11. Bolzano/Bozen - See the "Selva/ Wolkenstein" chapter, Excursion #3.

Directions: By car - Drive south out of Baselga, following signs to Trento. Pick up *autostrada* A22 to Bolzano. Reverse directions to return.

12. Venice - See the chapter on "Venice" for details.

Directions: By car - Drive south from town to #47 east, then south through Bassano to the outskirts of Padua where you pick up E70 *autostrada* to Venice. You'll go over a long causeway and arrive at a busy and confusing area, the Piazza Roma, a dead end for car traffic. On your right is a pair of large, eight-story garages where you can park. There can be a long line of cars trying to get into these garages if you don't arrive by 9:00 am, but a tip might help. Walk from the garage across the top of Piazza Roma to the Grand Canal piers and take the large, inexpensive, public water-bus (Vaporetto) to San Marco. Reverse directions to return.

13. Egna/Neumarkt - See the "Vigo di Fassa" chapter, Excursion #8.

Directions: By car - Drive south towards Trento, picking up *autostrada* A22 towards Bolzano. Exit at Ora - Egna and turn south to Neumarkt/Egna. Reverse directions to return.

14. Belluno - See the "Cortina d'Ampezzo" chapter, Excursion #14.

Directions: By car - Drive south out of Baselga to #47. Drive east to #50, following signs to Belluno. Reverse directions to return.

Baselga di Pinè Walks

Recommended Maps:
1) Kompass - Carta Turistica #075 - Altopiano di Pinè
2) Carta Turistica - Altopiano di Pinè, Valle di Cembra

Walk #1: Introductory Walk around Lake Serraia and Lake Piazze

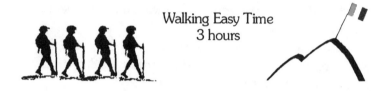

Walking Easy Time
3 hours

The walk around Baselga's lakes—Serraia and Piazze—can be taken on the afternoon of the day of your arrival. It serves as a nice introduction to the Baselga area and is a gentle walk that can be extended, if you follow the map.

Start: Visit the helpful Tourist Office on Baselga's main street and walk around the right side of the lake along *passeggiata #9*. Note the Bosco Negro, the forest high up on your right, the location of a hike you will be taking on another day. Continue walking on this gentle path, past the second lake of Piazze, turning left around the end of the lake to the village of Zaiini at 3432 ft. (1046 m.). (It is possible to extend the walk by turning right at the end of Lake Piazze on path #15, ascending through the woods to Castellani or Regnana, and turning left down towards the village of Piazze, into Zaiini.)

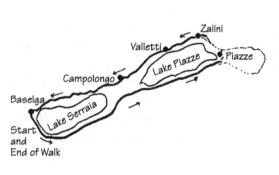

Continue south from Zaiini along the lake *passeggiata* through Campolongo at 3435 ft. (1047 m.). The mountain up on your right is the location of a hike to be taken on another day. Walk along Lake Serraia and into Baselga.

Walk #2: Baselga to Ricaldo to La Capannina to Bellevista to Baselga

Walking Easy Time
2½ hours

Today you will walk from the beginning of Lake Serraia at 3238 ft. (987 m.), through the hamlet of Ricaldo, continuing on a little-used auto road, easily and gradually ascending to 3809 ft. (1161 m.) and a popular picnic and sporting area. The path becomes a nice carriage road through the pine forest and brings you to some great views of the Cembra Valley, turning south on the same *Walking Easy* path and leading to a scenic viewpoint signed "Bellevista." It is gently downhill all the way to Baselga, through "old Baselga" with its narrow, cobblestone streets and old stucco houses. Once here you can pay a visit to two ancient churches.

Start: From the Tourist Information Office in Baselga, you will walk to Lake Serraia. Cross the street to the left, following the sign "Ricaldo 0,5 m," and walk up the hill on the right-hand cobblestone street through Ricaldo. After a few minutes you will reach the community bulletin board. Just past this little plaza, two auto roads go to the right. Take the upper one marked with the sign "escluso i frontisti." Follow the road up, arriving at a house on the right marked 62. Turn sharply left up the hill where you will see a yellow sign on the side wall of a building confirming your direction on Passeggiata #8, Bellevista. There is also a sign for cars

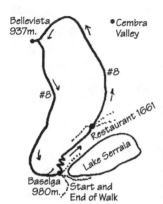

Bellevista 937m.
•Cembra Valley
#8
#8
Restaurant 1661
Lake Serrala
Baselga 980m.
Start and End of Walk

marked "Campo Sportivo." This road climbs steadily but gently.

After about 40 minutes you will come to a large, open plateau with sporting fields, picnic tables and the La Capannina restaurant. Walk across the plateau, passing the restaurant on your left, to the carriage path that is closed to auto traffic, indicating Passieggiata #8, Bellevista. This path descends and ascends very gently through the quiet pine forest. Before the trail turns to the left, notice the great views of the Cembra Valley.

As you turn south to return to Baselga, a sign takes you for a short walk to the right to Bellevista, for more remarkable country scenes. When ready, return to the carriage road and continue down towards Baselga. When the carriage path ends, take the auto road down to the right, into "old Baselga," heading for the steeple of the Church of S. Maria Assunta. Many of the old stucco houses still have vestiges of their ancient fresco colors and they offer some great photographic opportunities. This church dates back to the 13th century, but its origins may be even older. Note the Gothic-style apse with three triforium windows of local stone. Continue down to another beautiful white church and turn left on the road in front of the second church, walking into Baselga, where you began today's walk.

Walk #3: Excursion to Montagnaga, Bernardi to Madonnina di Pinè to Buss to Guarda to Puel to Bernardi

Walking Easy Time
3 hours

This mostly level walk is in the forests, meadows and fields south of Baselga and includes a short but interesting stop at the little village of Montagnaga. There you will visit the Parish Church of S. Anna, dedicated to the Madonna of Caravaggio. The church, with its magnificent, restored paintings, was raised to the status of a "Marian sanctuary" after the appearance of the Madonna to the shepherd girl Domenica Targa in 1729. Note the votive offering room with its many plaques attesting to the graces conceded by the Madonna. Follow the signs to the Comparsa, indicating the location of the visitation. In the Comparsa are two bronze, life-size figures representing this scene. On the hill next to the Comparsa is a Monument to the Redeemer, a gift of the diocese commemorating the mystery of the Redemption.

A mountain road will take you west of Montagnana, just up the hill to the hamlet of Bernardi at 3150 ft. (960 m.), where the walk begins on green route #5. This well-signed, gentle, unspoiled forest path leads around to Madonnina di Pinè, a small forest shrine, and continues south to Buss at 2559 ft. (780 m.) and up to Guarda at 2855 ft. (870 m.), returning to Bernardi through the meadows and forest at Puel. While there are not many extraordinary views from the trail, the comfortable path is peaceful and pleasant.

Directions: Drive south from the 2 Camini Hotel and bear right at the signed entrance to the village of Montagnana. Park the car near the church and Comparsa for visits before starting the walk. When ready, drive back up the artistically cobblestoned street and make a left turn up the hill past the sign for Bernardi. Make another left turn into the parking area of the Albergo San Giorgio (the only place to park in the village).

Start: Return to the auto road you just drove up on and walk up the hill, making your first left turn past the little chapel, going by some very old houses. Make a right turn and walk on the lower of the two roads, following the sign to Bernardi-Madonnina di Pinè, *passeggiata* #5, heading in a northerly direction. The road becomes a comfortable wagon path as it turns into the forest. This gentle path continues to be well-marked, and after a while you will arrive at an intersection—make a right turn in the signed direction of the little chapel Madonnina di Pinè, only a one-third-mile (.6 km) detour.

When ready, return to the original path, ascending to the right in the direction of Puel. This forest trail leads you all the way into Buss, across a road and to the left, eventually turning north and ascending in the direction of Guarda at 2881 ft. (878 m.). The path goes by some houses on the road to a large open meadow and fields, continuing to the right (north) on a small, signed carriageway, back into Bernardi and the little chapel you passed earlier. Turn right and walk down the road to where you parked your car.

Walk #4: Piazzo (through the Vineyards) to Faver to Piazzo, Excursion to Earth Pyramids of Segonzano

Walking Easy Time
3 to 5 hours

Reserve the day for this remarkable trip—it will probably be the highlight of your Baselga *Walking Easy* holiday!

You'll enjoy today's walks, but it is the views that will astound you. You will leave by car for the 20-minute drive to the ancient hamlet of Piazzo, easily found on the road to Cembra. Piazzo is so small that you will have to park your car near the church (there is no other available space), where the first part of today's walk begins. After exploring this tiny community, which probably hasn't changed much over hundreds of years, you will walk through the terraced vineyards and fruit orchards, and if you visit the Cembra Valley in mid-September, the grapes and apples will be almost ready for harvest. One can't help being overwhelmed by this tranquil but magnificent scene, as the valley floor rises almost vertically, every square foot on the hillsides bursting with grapes, and their famous golden and red apples.

The vineyard path goes into the forest on a narrow trail that ascends easily to the village of Faver at 2208 ft. (673 m.). Here you can make a quick visit, returning to Piazzo on the same path, through the forest and vineyards, for a second perspective. The ruins of the Castle of Segonzano are up on the mountainside, in full view of the path. The town fathers have arranged for the history of the castle, as well as other important local facts, to be printed in Italian and English along the way, and if you wish, the walk up to the ruins is clearly signed and not very far.

After returning to your car, you will start off for the second part of today's excursion, a walk and visit to the Earth Pyramids of Segonzano. Glaciers left enormous deposits of sediment, as well as stones and large blocks in the valley. In the course of millenia, erosion gave rise to the formation of the pyramids, mounds of earth balancing large blocks and stones at their peaks. You will have the opportunity of walking up to groups of these amazing pyramids, close enough to touch them!

Directions: Leave Baselga by car in the direction of Trento. Stay on this road, passing the turn to S. Mauro, and after a hairpin turn take the first road leading off sharply to the right, signed for Segonzano and descending into the valley. Turn right at the major auto road, past Lases, Lona and Sevignano, and turn left at the sign to Cembra and Faver. After a short while, watch for the signed mountain road on the right to the hamlet of Piazzo. Drive up the hill and turn sharply right, parking at the church in Piazzo. **Do not attempt to drive in Piazzo!** Pay a visit to the lovely, restored 12th-century church.

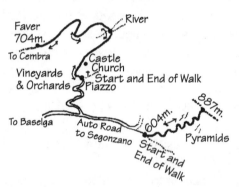

Start: Walk down and away from the church, turning right at the little grocery store on your right. (There are E5 signs near the church— they take you up to the pyramids and to Baselga—do **not** follow this path.) Follow the narrow, cobblestone street to the left, facing the grocery store, which eventually will be marked E5 and blazed red and white.

After a few meters, a sign on the right points up the hill to the impressive ruins of Segonzano Castle, which you may want to visit on the way back. During the nearly 600 years of its history, this castle experienced many important events and saw many ruling lords come and go. It was seriously damaged during the French occupation in the late 1700s, was abandoned and never restored. Continue on the little road marked E5, walking through fruit orchards and vineyards, with views of the tightly terraced mountainside. Sitting on top of the mountain is the steeple of the church at Faver and, further to the left, the ancient village of Cembra.

Proceed down the narrow, little-used auto road and turn left over the bridge, following the sign for E5: Sentieri Europeo, Faver, and Lago Santo. On the right are blocks of porphyry, placed there in honor of the great German painter Albrecht Duerer, with A.D. 1471 inscribed on them. They were placed here in 1971 by Baron Silvio a Prato, a patron of the arts, to commemorate the 500th anniversary of the birth of this famous painter who visited the Cembra Valley on his way to Venice in 1494. Duerer was impressed by the Segonzano area and immortalized it in his famous watercolor "Alpine Countryside." In Faver he painted "Alpine Castle" and from the road below, the watercolor "Castle Ruins on the Rocks."

Follow the signed, ascending trail into the forest in the direction of Faver. This trail winds around the end of the valley, still marked E5, and emerges at 2231 ft. (680 m.), into the ancient village of Faver. It is possible to walk along the road into Cembra, the major village of the Cembra Valley, but it is probably a better idea to stop at Faver. After taking in the views, return down the same path you came up on, walking back through the orchards and vine-yards for a new perspective, to your car at the church in Piazzo.

For the second half of today's explorations, drive down to the main road, turning left and left again at the major intersection for the short drive to Segonzano. Park in the large area on the right signed "Piramidi di Segonzano." The path up to the pyramids is carefully engineered and signed, and rises from 1982 ft. (604 m.) to 2920 ft. (890 m.), if you wish to go all the way to the top. Segonzano is a very popular stop and the steps up can be crowded with visitors to this natural phenomenon.

You only have to walk up to Group II for sensational, close-up views of the earth pyramids, and to aid you in un-derstanding the pyramids, there are signs in English explaining the evolutionary process. Make sure you've brought enough film—the trip up is quite scenic. After about 30 to 40 minutes you will approach your destination, and a sign will direct you left to Group II. After viewing on the first platform, make sure you continue on the little path to the right to the second platform, for additional exciting exposures to the pyramids and a clear view of the Cembra Valley.

When ready, descend on the carefully maintained path to the parking area. Turn left on the auto road, passing the turn-off to Cembra you took earlier, and continuing through Sevignano, Lona, and Lases, finally making a left turn at the sign for Pinè. At the top of the hill turn left again, into Baselga.

Walk #5: Baselga to Lake Serraia to Lake Piazze through the Bosco Negro on Monte Costalta to Fovi to Baselga

Walking Easy Time
3 hours

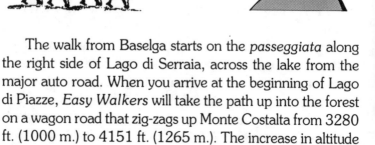

The walk from Baselga starts on the *passeggiata* along the right side of Lago di Serraia, across the lake from the major auto road. When you arrive at the beginning of Lago di Piazze, *Easy Walkers* will take the path up into the forest on a wagon road that zig-zags up Monte Costalta from 3280 ft. (1000 m.) to 4151 ft. (1265 m.). The increase in altitude of 870 ft. (265 m.) is not difficult when taken at a slow, easy pace.

The path begins to descend gradually as it goes through Bosco Negro (the "black forest"), still in the forest, all the way down to Fovi and a narrow, paved auto road at 3527 ft. (1075 m.). After passing through this little hamlet, you walk down through cornfields and berry farms to Lake Serraia and Baselga.

Start: Turn right on the *passeggiata* at the start of Lake Serraia, following path #9 along the lake, until you come to a four-way intersection before the second lake, Lake Piazza. Turn right on the **unsigned** path that climbs on a zig-zagging, well-defined wagon road through the forest. There are some side paths that dart in and out of the road—stay on the same wide path all the way.

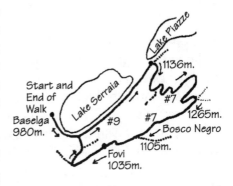

The path continues under the top of a ski lift, zig-zagging until 4151 ft. (1265 m.) at a four-way intersection with a little shrine on the left and a sign indicating where you came from (Serraia). Turn right on this **unmarked** wagon road which continues to be path #7, as you walk through the Bosco Negro forest. Note the signs pointing in the direction you came from—this walk was intended to be taken in the reverse direction. But you are still on path #7, now descending gently through the upscale community of Fovi and reaching a paved auto road.

Follow the road down, leaving Fovi, and turn right just before the ice rink, on a narrow, paved, little-used road through the cornfields and fruit farms for which the Altopiano di Pinè is noted. Turn left at the intersection, walking to Lake Serraia. Turn left again along the lake for the short walk into Baselga.

Walk #6: Baselga to Vigo (through the Laghestel) to Ferrari to Vigo to Baselga

Walking Easy Time
2¾ hours

Today's mostly level walk is marked #2 on your maps and goes through the protected forest reserve of Laghestel, south of Baselga di Pinè—a perfect introduction to the Altopiano di Pinè, the high plateau of the Pinè Valley. You will leave from the Hotel 2 Camini and walk up to the nearby village of Vigo, an unspoiled hilltop hamlet, and its 17th-century Church of St. Joseph. After visiting the church you will leave Vigo, walking through the berry farms and fruit orchards in the direction of Laghestel.

The walk through the nature reserve is mostly on a wagon path through pine woods interspersed among peat bog swamps. This protected area comprises a natural refuge and habitat for many species of plants and small animals. Many of the paths here are lined with blackberry bushes, and if you are walking in September they can be a delicious snack (remember the thorns, however). The trail returns around the protected forest, back to Ferrari and Vigo.

Start: At the Hotel Due (2) Camini, walk across the main auto road and up the side road towards the church tower and the hamlet of Vigo. At the village center and fountain, turn right and walk up a gravel path taking you to the high ground and the 17th-century church with its marvelous panorama of the Pinè Valley. Visit this small restored church with its old frescoes and lovely altar, noted for its frequent three-bell concerts by its accomplished *campanaro* (master bell ringer).

Return to village center, pass the bulletin board and make a right turn, entering the walking path through the fruit farms and orchards. This path comes to a small paved road. Turn right and note the old stone markers on your right, dated 1876 and marked "Via del Vigo." Follow the road to a gravel jeep road and a sign that announces Laghestel straight ahead.

Walk through the forest to the main sign welcoming you to Biotopo Natural Reserve Laghestel. As you walk through the quiet forest, stay right at the first two forks on the major carriage road. This path, *passeggiata #2*, is entirely in the cool forest and follows the perimeter of this natural, protected reserve. There are many side trails leading off the main path, so it is easy to become confused unless you remain on the main trail. The carriage way turns around the pine forest to the left, bringing you to a gently ascending trail, rising up through pine trees to an intersection. Stay left on this forest trail, do not descend on the trail to the right.

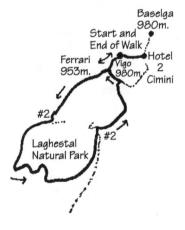

You will soon arrive at a jeep road, where you will find a Laghestel information map and a picnic table. It is **important** to turn left here, on the carriage road, in a northerly direction, to the park entrance/exit in Ferrari. You will exit at an auto road about 50 meters to the right of where you entered the park today. Cross the road, walking past the playground, then turn left at the little path and right again quickly at the intersection. Follow the country lane up to the square you visited earlier in Vigo, turning right at Vigo town center and descending to the Hotel 2 Camini.

HINT: There are many paths that intersect the main wagon road and it is quite easy to become confused. It might be a good idea to have your compass with you—remembering that a direction to the north returns you to the park entrance. Try to avoid extraneous routes through the forest, except as noted on the map.

VENICE

The proximity of the grand city of Venice to walking areas in the Italian Alps is a super bonus for *Easy Walkers*. It is only a two-hour drive on good roads from Cortina d'Ampezzo to the parking garages outside Venice. For those who prefer to avoid the hassle of Venice parking, bus tours are available from base villages leaving for Venice in early morning and returning the same evening. Check your local Tourist Office for current details.

This chapter is intended to provide *Easy Walkers* with an informative and casual **one-day** walking tour of Venice. However, you also should obtain a detailed street map of Venice, available at the Azienda di Promozione Turistica, conveniently located under the arcade in the far left corner of Piazza San Marco, your first stop in Venice. Chances are you'll get lost—make the most of it and enjoy!

☞ **HINT: All streets lead to and from the Piazza San Marco. Look overhead for directional signs back to the *piazza*.**

Transportation to Venice

Venice is linked to the rest of Italy by *autostrada*. By car from the Cortina d'Ampezzo area, take 51 south towards Belluno, following signs to *autostrada* A27, into Mestre and Venice. Drive over a causeway and you will arrive at a somewhat busy and confusing area, the Piazza Roma, a dead-end for car traffic. On the right is a pair of large parking garages for visitors' use. There can be long lines trying to get into these garages if you don't arrive before 9:00 am, but a tip to the garage attendant may help convince him to let you pass into the garage where parking is usually extremely tight. There are attendants inside the garage who will help you find a spot. Parking costs are between 20,000 to 40,000 lire ($14 to $28) per day, depending on the size of the car. (Please note that all prices quoted are as of summer 1994.)

> ☞ **HINT: Put all belongings inside your locked car trunk for safekeeping, and write down the location of the parking space and the floor.**

Walk from the garage across the top of Piazza Roma to the Grand Canal piers (follow the crowds) and take the large, inexpensive public water bus (Vaporetto), for an exciting canal ride. Get off at the San Marco stop.

> ☞ **HINT: Take Vaporetto #1 (the Grand Canal local) and try to sit in an outside seat for your first views of incredible Venice. It is possible to take more expensive, alternative water transportation, but although the vaporetto takes a little longer, it serves as a fine introduction to the sights and sounds of Venice.**

Transportation in Venice

1) Vaporetti circle the city and run the length of the Grand Canal, with 20 different lines or routes. Line 5 circles Venice and stops at the islands of Murano and the Guidecca. Line 2 is an express connecting the train station to the Rialto Bridge, the Lido and San Marco. Line 1 is the Grand Canal local. Timetables and ticket booths are at each stop. The cost is 2200 lire on most lines, 3300 lire for express lines—unless you buy discount passes, such as the **Tourist Ticket (Biglietto Turistico)**. This 24-hour pass, costing 13,000 lire ($7), allows one-day travel on any route of the city's Vaporetti. A three-day ticket costs 22,000 lire ($13). Average fare on a local line making every stop (*accelerato*) is 2200 lire; on the lines making only express stops (*diretto*), the fare is 3300 lire. Use these figures to decide if buying a discount ticket is economical for the time you will be in Venice.

2) Motoscafi are sleek motorboats or water-taxis, and are very expensive. **Always** agree on a set fare before beginning the trip—50,000 lire ($32) is the minimum price and doesn't take you very far.

3) Traghetti are a well-kept secret, used by many locals. They are two-person gondolas that ferry people across the Grand Canal at different points—the cheapest and shortest of the gondola rides—for 500 lire. Look for their signs along the Grand Canal.

4) Gondola rides in the late afternoon are a romantic, if expensive, way to see Venice's canals. Gondoliers usually charge 70,000 lire for up to five people, higher after 8:00 pm. Bargaining is expected.

Easy Walkers' "Must See" Venice

1) The Grand Canal Tour - Vaporetto Line 1 at San Marco landing can take *Easy Walkers* on a leisurely cruise of Venice's main waterway, looping two miles through the city—red-and-white-striped gondola boat moorings along the way. A seat in the prow will give a clear view of the sights—three bridges and almost 200 palaces built from the 14th to the 18th centuries.

Leaving San Marco, at left is the large, white, domed, 17th-century baroque church of **Santa Maria della Salute**. Next is the **Palazzo Venier dei Leoni**, housing the **Peggy Guggenheim Collection of 20th Century Painting and Sculpture**. The **Gritti Palace Hotel** is across the canal on the right bank along with the Renaissance palace **Ca'Grande**. Just before the **Accademia Bridge** is **Palazzo Barbaro**, where author Henry James lived and wrote. This wooden bridge dates back only to 1934 and leads to the fabulous **Accademia Gallery.**

On the left bank, a few minutes past the bridge, note the baroque mansion **Ca'Rezzonico**, poet Robert Browning's last residence. Further along on the left is the **Museum of 18th Century Venice (Museo del Settencento Veneziano)** with fine Venetian paintings by Guardi, Longhi, Tiepolo, etc. On the left bank, the boat passes two identical 15th-century Gothic palaces, one the home of Richard Wagner where he wrote "Tristan und Isolde."

Rounding a bend in the canal, note **Palazzi Mocenigo** on the right bank, four buildings with lion's heads (where Byron lived while writing "Don Juan"), then look for the Renaissance palaces **Palazzo Corner-Spinelli** and **Palazzo Grimani**, also on the right bank. Approaching the **Rialto Bridge** the canal narrows, and just beyond it, on the right, is the Gothic **Ca' d'Oro**, housing the **Franchetti Gallery**, with its collection of tapestries, sculptures and paintings.

A little further down, on the left bank, are two museums, the **Galleria d'Arte Moderna** and **Museo Orientale**, housed in the Baroque palace of **Ca' Pesaro**. Also on the left is the white church **San Stae**, and if you exit the boat here you'll walk through local neighborhoods filled with the trappings of day-to-day Venetian life. However, be aware that street names change and numbers often don't seem to follow in any order. Back on the boat, on the right bank is the Renaissance **Palazzo Vendramin-Calergi**, where Wagner died in 1883, now housing the **Casino** in winter.

2) Piazza di San Marco Area - Get off the Vaporetto at **San Marco** and walk straight ahead through the **Piazzetta** (the entrance to St. Mark's Square). Two columns face the waterfront here—one topped by a winged lion and the other with St. Theodore and his dragon.

The **Doge's Palace (Palazzo Ducale)** rises in pink-and-white marble splendor above the Piazzetta. The palace was not only the Doge's residence, but it also served as Parliament, Law Courts and the Prison. Enter the palace through the ornate 15th-century **Gate of the Paper (Porta della Carta)** into a large courtyard. Ahead you can see the **Stairway of the Giants (Scala dei Giganti)**, flanked by immense statues of Neptune and Mars. To reach the rooms open to the public, walk along the arcade to a central staircase leading to the **Anticollegio**, with paintings by Tintoretto and Veronese. The world's largest oil painting, "Paradise" by Tintoretto, hangs in the **Great Council Hall**. Guided tours, in Italian only however, are available to view the palace's secret rooms. The **Bridge of Sighs (Ponte dei Sospiri)** is located outside the east wing of the palace. Leading to the prison, the bridge was given its name because of the sighs of prisoners being taken to their jails. The Palace is open daily from 8:30 am to 6:00 pm, with an admission charge.

Continue into **St. Mark's Square**, passing the **Bell Tower (Campanile di San Marco)** on your left. The bell in the tower, the Marangona, peals at sunrise, noon and sunset. There is usually a long line of visitors waiting at the elevator which rises to the top of the Tower with its panoramic views of Venice—you might wish to spend your limited time elsewhere unless you can get in quickly. The tower is open daily from 9:15 am to 8:30 pm, and there is an admission charge.

Directly in front of you, on a building facade, is the animated clock **Torre dell'Orologia**, built in 1496, with Moorish figures that strike on the hour. The clock tells the time while matching the signs of the zodiac to the position of the sun. Unfortunately, the interior of the tower is now closed for safety reasons.

To the right of the Clock Tower is **Saint Mark's Basilica (Basilica di San Marco)**. The church was built from 1063 to 1073 and remodelled in a variety of styles. It is the Piazza's treasure, considered one of Europe's most beautiful churches, and is laid out in a Greek cross topped by five domes—a mix of Byzantine and Romanesque styles. Visit the **Atrium** with its six mosaic cupolas depicting scenes from the Old Testament; the **Basilica** with a stunning composition of marble, alabaster, and mosaics; and the **Baptistry** with its dominating baptismal font. The **Treasury** (open Monday through Saturday from 9:30 am to 5:30 pm and from Sunday 2:00 to 5:00 pm) and the **Presbytery**, with the Byzantine "Pala d'Oro" of gold and gemstones from Constantinople, considered the most valuable treasure of the church, are fascinating and open to the public with an admission charge.

The atrium stairs outside the basilica lead to the **Marciano Museum** with "Quadriga," four horses yoked together, cast in the 4th century, and brought to Venice from Constantinople by crusaders in the early 13th century. The museum is open Monday through Saturday from 10:00 am to 5:30 pm and Sunday 2:00 to 4:30 pm, and there is an admission charge. Admission to the church itself is free, however, and there is an English-speaking tour at 11:00 am, Monday through Saturday.

> ☞ **HINT: Guards in the Piazza di San Marco area are strict and turn away improperly dressed visitors (those without shirts or wearing shorts, halter or tank tops, or sleeveless blouses).**

The **Museo Correr**, at the far end of the piazza, is open from 10:00 am to 4:00 pm daily, Sundays 10:00 am to 12:30 pm, and is closed Tuesdays. It houses a priceless collection of paintings, sculpture, ancient documents, clothing and currency.

Walk outside in **St. Mark's Square** for fabulous views of the Basilica and the Palace. Thousands of people compete for space with the pigeons, while colorful cafés provide live orchestras, cappuccino, and a comfortable (although expensive) place to view the passing parade. The streets around the square are filled with typical tourist stores, *trattorias* and fine restaurants, and elegant boutiques including Fendi, Armani, Valentino, Gucci, Cartier, Hermès and Missoni. Most restaurants are good, though generally expensive, many specializing in local seafood—check the menu before entering.

3) Accademia Gallery - Leave the far end of St. Mark's Square, near the Tourist Information Office, and walk towards Campo Morosini, also known as Campo San Stefano. Turn left to cross the canal on the Accademia Bridge to reach the Accademia Gallery. This art museum houses an impressive collection of Venetian paintings including works by Canaletto, Bellini, Tinteretto, Mantegna, Carpaccio, Giorgione and Titian. Hours are Monday to Saturday, 9:00 am to 2:00 pm, Sunday 9:00 am to 1:00 pm, and there is an admission charge.

4) The Peggy Guggenheim Collection is housed at the **Palazzo Venier dei Leoni**, a select museum of 20th-century painting and sculpture. Hours are Sunday, Monday, Wednesday and Friday from 11:00 am to 6:00 pm, Saturday 11:00 am to 9:00 pm, with an admission charge, but Saturday evenings are free. The gallery can be reached by following signs over the Accademia Bridge, one of only three bridges over the Grand Canal, or by taking a Traghetto to cross the canal.

5) Rialto Bridge (Ponte di Rialto), built in the late 16th century, was constructed with arches high over the canal to allow ancient, high-masted galleys to pass under it. The bridge is lined with windows of the stores inside. Vegetable, fish and fruit markets are on one bank of the bridge and chic boutiqes are on the other. Leave St. Mark's Square adjacent to the animated clock, bearing diagonally to your right, and follow the overhead signs through the maze of streets to the Rialto Bridge.

ACCOMMODATIONS

The following three- and four-star Italian hotels have been used by the authors on their walking trips. All rooms have private facilities, include full buffet breakfast (unless otherwise indicated), and are comfortable, scrupulously clean and well-located. Most hotels are family-owned and justifiably proud of their kitchens.

Note that when calling or faxing Italy, the international access number from the United States is always **011 39**, dialed first, followed by the listed telephone or fax number.

☞ **HINT: While these recommended hotels accept credit cards, please note that this is not the case with all European lodgings.**

ALLEGHE
Sporthotel Europa
Three-star; Owners - Efrem and Carla Case
32022 Alleghe
Tel: 437-523362, Fax: 437-723906
The Sporthotel Europa is located on lovely Lake Alleghe, its front rooms overlooking the trout-filled lake, the side bedrooms facing the wondrous wall of Mt. Civetta. The hotel has 30 bedrooms, all with modern, private facilities, and was rebuilt in 1979 by the present owners. The high incidence of repeat guests, both in summer and winter, attests to the quality of care and attention of the Case family, including daughters Giovanna and Caterina. The comfortable public rooms, filled with an abundance of fresh flowers, are used in

the evening by guests playing cards and games, reading, or just relaxing with fellow vacationers.

Breakfast is a bountiful buffet with juices, cereals, cheeses, meats, cold cereal and cake filling out an assortment of bread and rolls. Dinner includes a choice of three appetizers, three main dishes, a small fresh salad bar, and dessert. The chefs, who have been with the hotel over ten years, appeal to all palates with dishes from *risotto* with mushrooms to *spaghetti carbonara*. Each week in the summer a picnic is held at Piana di Pezzi (the mid-station of the Alleghe lift) with *antipasto*, salad, pasta, grilled meats, fruit, dessert and other tempting goodies! The Case family is very much in evidence at the Europa—a hotel on the edge of little-known Lake Alleghe—a hotel with comfortable rooms, warm ambience, good cooking, obliging staff, and caring owners.

BASELGA DI PINÈ
Hotel Due Camini
Three-star; Owners - Lucia and Franca Merz
38042 Baselga di Pinè
Tel: 461-557200, Fax: 461-558833

This small hotel takes its name from its two large fireplaces, one in the formal dining room and one in the combination public room, bar and informal dining area. The original building was constructed as a restaurant in 1974, to showcase the talents of chef "Mama Lucia," an acknowledged expert in the country cooking of the Trento region. In 1983, ten comfortable rooms with private facilities were added, managed by daughter Franca. The bedrooms feature pine panelling on walls and ceilings, complimenting the fine cuisine served in the dining room.

Hotel guests on demi-pension are not required to choose from a set menu—Franca will skillfully guide you to a choice of first course of soups or pastas, main course of meat/fish with vegetables, salad, and dessert—depending on what Signora Lucia has prepared in the kitchen. One of the local specialties you might try is *polenta* with a variety of sautéed mushrooms, served with slices of Vezzena cheese (a local Asiago similar to aged Vermont cheddar), and for dessert, fresh peach pie or local raspberries and strawberries. Breakfast is basically continental, with juice, rolls and butter and jam, and hot beverages, in addition to cold cereal.

The comfortable surroundings and delicious food have brought guests back to the Due Camini season after season, some for 20 years. The restaurant is rated two forks in the "Michelin Guide" and is well-received in the "Osteria D'Italia" or "slow food guide" (as opposed to fast foods), and is probably the finest restaurant in the area. Lucia speaks Italian and French, but Franca's English is excellent and she is a font of information—from where to get your hair cut in Milan to the history of the neighboring Valle dei Mocheni. Baselga di Pinè and the Due Camini Restaurant/Hotel have not been discovered by American walkers/tourists...yet!

CORTINA D'AMPEZZO

Savoia Grand Hotel
Four-star; Manager - Maurizio Pretto
Via Roma, 62, 32043 Cortina d'Ampezzo
Tel: 436-3201, Fax: 436-2731

The Savoia Grand Hotel has a long history in Cortina d'Ampezzo, opening in 1924 as one of the grand, society hotels and boasting such illustrious guests as Franklin Roosevelt, Jr., Prince Umberto (before he became king) of Italy, and countless other famous personalities. The hotel, now with 63 rooms, boasts a high percentage of returning guests each year. Many staff members have been with the hotel for 15 to 20 seasons, and Mr. Pretto, the manager, has been in residence for over six years. Knowledgable concierges can help you with everything from hiking path suggestions to restaurant reservations.

The formally decorated yet comfortable public rooms are used for card-playing, reading and conversation and add a grandeur not found in the usual *Easy Walker* base village hotel, and the dining and bar service are worthy of a four-star hotel. Unlike most other areas in the Italian Alps, Cortina is a chic, expensive town—you might want to pamper yourself and enjoy this grand old hotel in a quiet part of town, away from the throngs of visitors on the pedestrian street.

Across the street from the Savoia Grand, in its park-like setting, is a building erected in 1937, closed in 1991, connected to the Savoia by underground tunnel. It is undergoing renovation and will be opened in the winter of '94/'95 as a bed and breakfast, with its own facilities and a pool on the roof—an alternative that *Easy Walkers* might consider.

MERANO

Hotel Minerva
Three-star; Directors - Peter and Adriana Castelforte
39012 Merano
Tel: 473-230460, Fax: 473-236712

Like a stately dowager, the 85-year-old Hotel Minerva has managed to retain her charm, dignity and beauty, due in no small part to the caring directorship of Peter and Adriana Castelforte. The 45 bedrooms are commodious and comfortable, bright and airy because of the high ceilings. Room 329 is a delight, with a balcony and a bathroom large enough to accommodate a small apartment! The public rooms, with a bar, card tables, and comfortable chairs and sofas, are conducive to afternoon tea, evening aperitif, reading, writing letters or discussions about the best trails from the Meranerhütte. The kitchen is excellent—the chef of five years prepares many Südtirolean as well as Italian specialties—and an evening salad bar and morning breakfast buffet help ensure a high percentage of return guests (50% in some seasons).

On a warm sunny day, the secluded swimming pool, bordered by fruit trees and grape arbors, is a great place to relax. The flowers and trees on the hotel grounds are lovely, well-tended, and add to the Mediterranean atmosphere cultivated in Merano. This grand old hotel is located in the lovely Maia Alta section of Merano, only a ten-minute walk into town, with bus service to many walking areas practically at the doorstep of the hotel. The Castelfortes manage a comfortable, caring establishment where *Easy Walkers* will feel right at home.

SELVA/WOLKENSTEIN   6 l(39

Hotel Malleier
Three-star; Owner - Elmar Torggler
39048 Selva/Wolkenstein
Tel: 471-795296, Fax: 471-794364

The chalet-style Hotel Malleier, situated on a quiet street above the village of Selva, offers wonderful views of the Sella mountain group, the Langkofel and Cir peaks, from its rooms and the sunny garden patio. Elmar Torggler has owned the hotel for 25 years and, with his brother ensconced in the kitchen as chef and a young, caring staff, has made the Malleier a family hotel with many satisfied return guests. The 35 comfortable bedrooms have modern, private facilities, balconies, and down comforters to sink into on cool mountain evenings, and Mr. Torggler has informed us that the hotel will undergo renovations to create even more comfortable surroundings for his guests.

The Tyrolean buffet breakfasts set the standard for the day—cold meats and cheeses, yoghurts, cold cereals, a dozen kinds of bread, rolls and cakes, pots of preserves, canned fruit, and of course, hot beverage of choice. Dinners reflect the local cuisine—a mixture of northern Italian and Austrian specialities—and dishes range from *polenta* to *spaghetti carbonara* to *weiner schnitzel*! There are usually four courses plus a salad, and the kitchen is very accommodating to the requests of anyone who would prefer a substitute.

In the evening, the public rooms are filled with satisfied guests playing cards, reading, talking and discussing the next day's activities. The hotel is away from the hustle and bustle of Selva's main street, but close to lifts, buses and walking trails. Note that the last two weeks of June and the months of July and September, are wonderful hiking times—the lifts are open and these periods avoid national vacation times in Italy and France, so the area is quieter. Mr. Torggler assures us that *Easy Walkers* will be welcomed warmly at any time, but especially during those less-hectic months.

VIGO DI FASSA
Hotel Cima Dodici
Three-star; Owners - Vito, Pierino and Mario Cassari
38039 Vigo di Fassa
Tel: 462-64175, Fax: 462-63540

The owners of chalet-style Cima Dodici since 1963 are father Vito, and two sons Pierino and Mario. The original hotel was built in 1956, renovated in 1966 and 1969, with the last major construction in 1988 when the bar area and the entire ground floor were remodelled. The 32 rooms in the hotel, located in a quiet section of town, are quite comfortable, with ample closet space, balconies and private facilities. The public rooms in the bar area are well-used, especially after dinner, when families congregate for their evening cappuccino, games, cards and good conversation.

The kitchen, under the supervision of chef Mario, features excellent local cuisine with a first course of soup or pasta, second course of veal, etc., an excellent salad bar and a choice of dessert. The menu is posted every morning and the chef is quite accommodating if the main course is not to your liking. Breakfast is basically "continental" with juice, rolls and butter and jam, plain cake, and a hot beverage. Pierino's wife Maria and two daughters Daniela and Barbara, also work in the hotel, with Barbara the only one with even a smattering of English. However, with an Italian-English dictionary, many smiles, and a lot of *per favores* and *grazies*, you will get along just fine.

INDEX TO WALKS

Selva/Wolkenstein
Ciampinoi/Comici/Passo Sella/Sassolungo/Plan de Gralba .. 60
Dantercepies/Rif. Clark/Rif. Forcelles/Gardena/Plan 63
Parco Naturale Puez-Odle/Vallunga...................................... 66
Plan/Col Raiser/Gamsblut/St. Jakob/Ortesei 67
Ortesei Alpe di Siusi/Saltaria/St. Cristina 69
Ortesei/Ega di Cason/Rif. Brogles/Seceda 72
Ortesei/Seceda/Col Raiser... 73

Cortina d'Ampezzo
Introductory Walk along Passeggiata....................................89
Auronzo/Lavaredo/Tre Cimi Locatelli/Drei Zinnen Hütte 90
Triple Lift/Tofana di Mezzo/Col Drusci/Rif. Ghedina 92
Faloria/Rist. Rio Gere/Cristallo/Rif. Mietres/Rif. Tondo.......95
Col de Varda/Rif. Citta di Carpi/Lake Misurina circle 97
Scoiattoli/Averau/Cinque Torri/Bái de Dónes 99
Lagazoi/Rif. Scotoni/Cabin Alpina/Lagazoi 102

Vigo di Fassa
Introductory Walk: Larzonei/Vallonga 114
Col Rodella/F. August/S. Pertini/Malga Sasso Piatto/Duron/
Campitello 116
Catinaccio/Ciampedie/Gardeccia/Vajolet/Pera di Sopra 118
Rosengarten/Paolina/Cristomannos/Lake Carezza 120
Catinaccio/Ciampedie/Negritella/Alta Via di Fassa 123
Canazei/Pecol/Belvedere/Lago di Fedaia/Marmolada 124
Rosengarten/Paolina/Cristomannos/Hirzlweg/Paolina 126
Passo San Pellegrino/Albergo Miralago/Fociade/Miralago .. 127
Moena/Canazei 128

Alleghe

Introductory Walk along Lago di Alleghe............................. 136
Col dei Baldi/Rif. Coldai/Lago Coldai/Col dei Baldi........... 137
Lago di Fedaia/Marmolada Glacier 139
Citta di Fiume/Malga Prendera along Alte Via Dolomiti 141
Rif. Staulanza/Rif. Venezia/Rif. Staulanza 144
Masarè/Sala/Forchiade/Masarè 146
Canale d'Agordo excursion/Val di Garès walk.................... 148
Rif. Falier/Marmolada Glacier excursion........................... 150

Meran/Merano

Algund along Algunder Waalweg/Tappeiner Weg 165
Piffing/Merano 2000/Meraner Hütte/Falzeben/Hafling 166
Hochmut/Tiroler Kreuz/S. Tirol/Brunnenberg/Dorf Tirol... 168
Forst/Lana/Marlinger Waalweg... 170
Hochmut/Longfallhof/Tiroler Kreuz/Dorf Tirol.................. 171
Dorf Tirol/Hochmut/Hans-Friedenweg/Leiter-Alm/Vellau.. 172
Merano/Schenna 173
Gilf Promenade 173
Passer River.. 173
Winter & Summer Promenades 173

Baselga di Pinè

Introductory Walk around Lake Serraia/Lake Piazze........... 186
Ricaldo/La Capannina/Bellevista....................................... 187
Montagnaga/Bernardi/Mad. di Pinè/Buss/Guarda/Puel 188
Piazzo/Faver/Segonzano Earth Pyramids excursion............ 190
Lake Serraia/Lake Piazze/Bosco Negro/Fovi 194
Vigo through Laghestal/Ferrari/Vigo 196

INDEX

A

Accademia Gallery 205
accommodations 207-213
(see also "hotels")
Agordine valley 129, 130
Agordo 130-133, 148
air travel 16
airports 16
Algund 165, 166
Alleghe 12, 13, 129-150
Alpe di Siusi 49, 55, 69-71
Alta Via Dolomiti 137-139, 141-143, 150
Altopiano di Pinè 176, 196
Ampezzo valley 75
Anello Zoldano Trail 144, 145
apartments, renting 23
Auronzo 90, 91

B

backpacks 32-34
Baselga di Pinè 13, 175-198
Bedollo 180
beer 28
Bellevista 187, 188
Belluno 87, 88
Belvedere 124, 125
Bernardi 188-190
beverages 27-29
Biotopo Natur. Reserve Laghestel 197, 198

Bolzano 18, 55, 56, 153
boots 31, 33
Bosco Negro 194, 195
Bozen, see "Bolzano"
Brenner Pass 17, 20
Bressanone 18, 56, 57
Brixen, see "Bressanone"
Bruneck, see "Brunico"
Brunico 86
Bullaccia 55
buses 20, 21
Buss 188-190

C

cable cars 21
camping 24
Campitello 103, 109, 116-118
Campolongo 186, 187
Canale d'Agordo 130, 148, 149
Canazai 103, 104, 109, 110, 124, 125, 135
cars
  gasoline 36
  renting 19
castles 52, 156, 180, 191, 192
Catinaccio 12, 118-121, 123, 126
Cembra valley 175, 176
chairlifts 21
Chiusa 18, 162
churches 52, 79, 80, 156, 177, 178

Ciampedie 103, 118, 119, 123
Ciampinoi 47, 49, 53, 60, 61
Cinque Torri 12, 82, 99-101
Civetta 12
Civezzano 180
clothing 30-35
coffee 28, 29
cogwheel railways 21
Col da Prà 120
Col de Varda 97-99
Col dei Baldi 137, 138
Col Druscie 92-94
Col Raiser 49, 54, 67-69, 73, 74
Col Rodella 103, 116-118
Col Tondo 82, 97
Colle Santa Lucia 133
consulates 36
Cortina d'Ampezzo 12, 13, 75-102
Corvara 134
credit cards 35
Cristallo 82, 95, 96
Customs 35, 36

D

Dantercepies 47, 49, 53, 63, 64
discounts, senior 22, 41
Dobbiaco 83
Dolomites 12, 13, 15

Dorf Tirol 168-173
driver's license 19
driving 19, 20
Duties 35, 36

E

Earth Pyramids of Se-
gonzano 179, 190-194
Ega di Cason 72, 73
Egna 112
electricity 36
embassies 36
emergency numbers 36

F

Falcade 113
Faloria 95, 96
Falzeben 166-168
farms 23
Fassa valley, see "Val
di Fassa"
Faver 190-193
Ferrari 197
ferrata 93
FlexiRail cards 21, 22
flowers 16
food 24-27, 29, 30
Forchiade 146, 147
Fornace 180
Forst 170, 171
Fovi 194, 195
funiculars 21
Funivia Catinaccio 107
funivie 21

G

Gamsblut 67-69
Garès 130, 148, 149
gasoline 36, 37
Glorenza 162, 163
Glurns, see "Glorenza"
gnocchi recipe 26

gondolas 21
government 37
Grand Canal 200-202
Guarda 188-190
Guggenheim, Peggy
Collection 205

H

Hafling 166-168
half-board 23
Hans-Friedenweg 172,
173
health 37, 40
hiking vocabulary 39
Hochmut 168-173
holidays 37, 38
hotels 23, 29 (see also
"accommodations")

I-J

Ifinger 166
Innichen, see "San Can-
dido"
inns, see "hotels"
Innsbruck, Austria 59, 60
insurance 19, 38
IVA 44
jackets 31, 32

K

Kilometric tickets 22
King Laurin 104
Klausen, see "Chiusa"

L

La Capannina 187, 188
Ladin 11, 103
Ladino 47, 48
Lagazuoi 82, 102
Laghestel 196-198
Lago Coldai 137

Lago di Alleghe 136
Lago di Carezza 120, 122
Lago di Fedaia 124,
125, 129, 139
Lago di Piazze 176,
186, 194, 195
Lago di Serraia 176,
186-188, 194, 195
Lake Misurina 88, 91,
92, 97-99
Lana 170, 171
Langental, see
"Vallunga"
language 11, 38, 39, 47
Larzonei 114, 115
laundry 35, 39
le Foppe 146
Leiter-Alm 172, 173
Lienz, Austria 77, 86, 87
liqueur 28
Longfallhof 171, 172
luggage 33, 34

M

Madonnina di Pinè 188-
190
mail 39, 40
Malga Ciapela 129, 150
Malga Prendera 141
Malga Sasso Piatto 116-
118
maps, road 20
Marlinger Waalweg
170, 171
Marmolada 124, 125,
129, 132, 139-141, 150
Masarè 146, 147
Mazzin 108
meals 29, 30
measurements 40
medications 40
Meida 119, 120
menu turistico 29
Meran 2000 166
Meran(o) 13, 151-174
Meraner Höhenweg 171

metric system 40
Mezzocorona 18
Mietres 82, 97
Milan 16
Miralago 127
Moena 104, 105, 108, 109, 127
money 40, 41
Mont Pic 49
Montagnaga 188, 189
Monte Costalta 194
Monte Pano 49
Monument Cristomannos 120-122, 126
motels 24
Mt. Civetta 129
Mt. Pelmo 144-146
Munich 16
museums 41, 80, 81, 158, 201-205

N

National Tourist Offices 43
Nature Reserve of Laghestel 179
Neumarkt, see "Egna"
newspapers 41

O

Ora 18
Ortesei 48, 49, 54, 67-74

P

packing 33-35
packs 32-34
Padua 184, 185
Palazzo Ducale 203
Paolina 126
Parco Naturale Dolomiti di Sesto 84
Parco Naturale Puez-Odle 58, 66, 67

Passeiertal 153
Passo di Fedaia 139, 140
Passo Falzerago 99-102
Passo Gardena 48, 63-65
Passo Giau 150
Passo Pordoi 104
Passo San Pellegrino 127
Passo Sella 48, 104
Passo Staulanza 144
passport 41
Pecol 124, 125
Pera di Sopra 118-120
Pian 141
Pian di Pezzè 132, 137, 138
Piazza di San Marco 202-205
Piazza Roma 199, 200
Piazze 186
Piazzo 190-193
picknicking 30
Pieve di Cadore 83
Piffing 166-168
Pinè valley 175
Plan 63-65
Plan da Tieja 67-69
Plan de Gralba 49, 62
Pocol 82, 83, 100, 101
police 36
Ponte di Rialto 205, 206
Ponte Gardena 57, 58
Pozza di Fassa 107, 108, 119, 120
Puel 188-190
Puez-Odle 66, 67

R

rack and pinion railways 21
rail passes 21-23
Raschötz 55, 72, 73
recipes 25
restaurants 29, 30
restrooms 42

Rialto Bridge, see "Ponte di Rialto"
Ricaldo 187
Riffian 160
Riva del Garda 180, 181
Rocca Pietore 130
Rosengarten, see "Catinaccio"
Rovereto 111, 112

S

S. Giovanni di Fassa 110
Sala 146, 147
Saltaria 69-71
San Candido 84
San Mauro di Pinè 179, 180
Santa Cristina 49, 69-71
Sassolungo 12, 47, 60-62
Schenna/Scena 160, 173
Schloss Brunnenberg 168, 169
Schloss Tirol 168, 169
Seceda 55, 72-74
seggiovie 21
Segonzano 193
Seiser Alm, see "Alpe di Siusi"
Sella 47, 48, 104
Selva 12, 13, 47-74
Selva di Cadore 133, 141-144
senior discounts 22, 41
Sesto 84, 85
Sexten, see "Sesto"
shoes 31
shopping 42
Silver card 22
Soraga 108
South Tyrol, see "Südtirol"
St. Jakob 67-69
St. Mark's Square 203-205

St. Moritz, Switzerland 163, 164
St. Ulrich, see "Ortesei"
Sterzing, see "Vipiteno"
Südtirol 11-13, 151-153

T

Talbauer 168-172
Tappeiner Weg 152, 165, 166
telephone 42
time, European 42, 43
timing, travel 15, 16, 50
tipping 30, 43
tiramisù recipe 25
Tiroler Kreuz 168-172
Toblach, see "Dobbiaco"
Tofana di Mezzo 81, 82, 92-94
Tondi di Faloria 81
Tondo 95-97
Tourist Information Offices 43
trains 17-18
transportation
  air 16
  bus 20, 21

car 19, 36
train 17-18
traveler's checks 44
Tre Cimi 12, 90-92
Tre Croce pass 90, 91
Trentino 175
Trento 18, 175, 181, 182

U-V

Ultental 153
Vajolet 118, 119
Val di Fassa 103, 104, 107-110, 128
Val di Garès 148, 149
Val Gardena 47-50
Vallunga 48, 66, 67, 114, 115
value added tax (VAT) 44
Vellau 172, 173
Venice 13, 16, 76, 199-206
Verona 182-184
Vigo 196, 197
Vigo di Fassa 12, 13, 103-128
Vipiteno 161, 162

vocabulary, foreign
  food 26, 27
  hiking/map 39
  Ladino 48
  trains 18

W

waalwege 151, 164, 165
walk classifications 14, 46
walking stick 33
water 29, 44
weather 15, 16
wine 27, 28, 153
Wolkenstein, see "Selva"

Z

Zaiini 186, 187
Zuel 89, 90

Our books are available in many bookstores. If you have difficulty finding them, you can order directly from Gateway Books by sending check or money order to:
Gateway Books, 2023 Clemens Road, Oakland CA 94602

Walking Easy in the Austrian Alps $10.95........................... _____

Walking Easy in the French Alps $11.95............................_____

Walking Easy in the Italian Alps $11.95............................_____

Walking Easy in the San Francisco Bay Area $11.95....... _____

Walking Easy in the Swiss Alps $10.95..............................._____

Postage & Handling
First book............................$1.90   _____
Each additional book..........1.00   _____
California residents add 8% sales tax   _____

Total $ _____

( ) I enclose my check or money order
( ) Please charge my credit card

Visa   Master Card   American Express

#_____Exp. Date _____

Name on Card _____

Telephone (   )_____
Please ship to:

Name _____

Address _____

City/State/Zip_____
Our books are shipped bookrate. Please allow 2 - 3 weeks for delivery. If you are not satisfied, the price of the book(s) will be refunded in full. (U. S. funds for all orders, please.)

We want your comments, your criticisms and your suggestions of additional walks, excursions and accommodations to include in future editions. Please mail them to us at 2023 Clemens Road, Oakland, CA 94602, fax them to (510) 530-0497 or e-mail them to donmerwin@aol.com

Notes

_____

_____

_____

_____

_____

_____

_____

_____

_____

_____

_____

_____

_____

_____

_____

_____

_____

_____

_____

_____

_____

_____

_____

Notes